Five One-Act Plays

MADE FOR A WOMAN, BACHELOR HOLIDAY, POWER LUNCH, THE M WORD and YOUR MOTHER'S BUTT

BY ALAN BALL

★

★

DRAMATISTS
PLAY SERVICE
INC.

THE M WORD was first produced at the Lucille Ball Festival
of New Comedy, Jamestown, New York, May 1991.

TABLE OF CONTENTS

Made for a Woman 5

Bachelor Holiday 19

Power Lunch 51

The M Word 85

Your Mother's Butt 97

MADE FOR A WOMAN

MADE FOR A WOMAN was first produced by Manhattan Class Company (Robert LuPone and Bernard Telsey, Executive Directors; W.D. Cantler, Associate Director), in New York City, on March 22, 1993. It was directed by Arnold J. Mungioli, produced by Kent Adams and the production manager was Joann Carollo. The cast was as follows:

CARLY .... Erica Gimpel
TRENT .... Eric LaRay Harvey

CHARACTERS

CARLY, a beautiful young woman, any race
TRENT, a handsome young man, any race

SETTING

A roomy Manhattan loft, sparsely furnished with expensive, trendy furniture. A leather easy chair next to a small table with a portable telephone on it. Another chair at a vanity with makeup mirror and cosmetics spread across its surface. A large, open window upstage.

This could be a space where people actually live; it could also be the set for a television commercial targeted to the vanishing breed of young, upscale consumers who still believe every aspect of their lives can and should be glamorous.

MADE FOR A WOMAN

Lights reveal Carly sitting at the vanity, applying makeup. She is young, beautiful, vital and alive. She wears torn jeans, a tank top, a black leather jacket and cowboy boots. She flirts with her reflection in the mirror, then gets up and skips around the loft, wildly tossing her hair and bursting into spontaneous laughter, like a fashion model in a television commercial. Abruptly she drops into the easy chair and smiles as if at a private joke. She picks up the phone and dials.

CARLY. Hello, AT&T? I'm so glad you're my long-distance company. It's hard, juggling a career and a relationship, and still finding private time for myself. You make it easier. You really understand me. You're like a sister. I'm going to send you a Hallmark card. *(Pause.)* This is Carly. No, I don't have a problem with my service. I love my service, and I love you. Why don't you come over? I'll make some General Foods International Coffee! *(Pause.)* Well, some time soon, then. I'll call you first thing next week. Bye! *(She frowns, jumps up and crosses to the vanity, shedding her leather jacket as she goes. She deftly rearranges her hair into a sexier, night-on-the-town look and puts on a pair of flashy, dangly earrings. This seems to make her happy. She jumps up and dances around for a while, then abruptly drops into the easy chair, picks up the phone and dials, kicking off her boots as she does so. As she dials.)* One — eight hundred — the card. *(Pause.)* Hello, American Express? I'd like to apply for membership. *(Assumes a more relaxed position.)* Well, I already have a card, but I'd like another one. No, not for another family member, for me. *(Pause.)* I already have a green card, an Optima card, a gold card and a platinum card. What else do you have? That's it? Well, can I have another gold card? Great. *(Pause.)* This is Carly. Oh, I'd rather not give you that information over the phone, that's so impersonal. Why don't you come over? I'll make some General Foods International Coffee! Well, we don't have to have that, we could have Folgers. *(Pause.)* Taster's Choice? *(Pause.)* Don't you have a break coming up? *(She suddenly hurls the phone across the room. She sits, fuming, then crosses to the vanity and applies a darker shade of lipstick. Irritated.)* I have a job too, but I'm not a maniac about it. *(Having applied the new lipstick shade, she puckers her lips insanely, staring at her reflection in the mirror.)* Me. Only better! *(She gets up and walks across the stage, shedding her jeans as she goes, leaving them in a pile on the floor, and exiting off-stage. A moment, then Trent enters from the opposite side of the stage. He is young, handsome, athletic. He wears a dark T-shirt, sweat-pants, sneakers, a denim jacket, and a pair of sunglasses which he never removes. He could easily have stepped out of the J. Crew catalog. He carries a paper bag. He crosses immediately to the mirror to check his appearance. Off.)* Trent? Is that you?

TRENT. Yo.

CARLY. Did you get my antiperspirant?

TRENT. I did. *(He digs through her stuff on top of the vanity, finds some hair gel and proceeds to restyle his hair. Carly enters, pulling up the straps on a sexy party dress she has changed into. She carries a pair of spike-heeled shoes.)*

CARLY. Is this too dressy?

TRENT. *(Not looking at her.)* Too dressy for what?

CARLY. I don't know. Where are we going?

TRENT. We're not going anywhere, Carly. We're scaling back, remember?

CARLY. Oh, right. Downsizing.

TRENT. *Right*sizing.

CARLY. Then what are we going to do?

TRENT. I don't know. *(Carly sits in the easy chair and puts on one of the spike-heeled shoes.)*

CARLY. Did you get my antiperspirant?

TRENT. Paper bag. *(She crosses to the vanity, wearing one shoe, and retrieves the paper bag.)*

CARLY. Because I do not want to perspire tonight, Trent. Nor do I want white powdery residue under my arms.

TRENT. Gross, I know. Is this cut too dated?
CARLY. And no harsh chemicals. I have a very special pH balance.
TRENT. This always happens to me. I achieve the look I'm going for right as it becomes tired.
CARLY. I'm not delicate, mind you. Well, I can be when I want to be. What I need is an antiperspirant that's strong enough for a man —
TRENT. Do you think I could do a buzz cut, or would I look like a Q-tip? Be honest.
CARLY. But made for a woman. *(She pulls out a pink box labeled "Mystique," about the size of a shoe box.)*
TRENT. I need a more muscular upper body to carry off a buzz cut, don't I. *(He strides off-stage purposefully. Carly opens the box and peers inside, confused. She pulls from inside the box a plethora of styrofoam packaging and tosses the box aside, like an impatient child on Christmas morning. Inside the styrofoam packaging, she finds a very small container of antiperspirant. She tosses the styrofoam packaging on the floor and stares at the container quizzically, then places it on her vanity and steps back, looking at it from different angles. Trent enters dragging a portable rowing machine behind him, which he sets up C.)*
CARLY. Trent.
TRENT. Yo.
CARLY. I thought I told you to get the largest size antiperspirant they had.
TRENT. I did.
CARLY. But that can't be. It just can't be.
TRENT. *(Irritated.)* What?
CARLY. Look. It's so small.
TRENT. *(Removes his denim jacket and tosses it on the floor.)* All I know is I asked for the largest size of Mystique antiperspirant and that is what they gave me. And, frankly, it was a little embarrassing, asking for such a feminine product by name. *(Mounts the rowing machine and begins to row.)* Good thing I'm secure in my masculinity.
CARLY. But it's barely enough to last me a week.
TRENT. Buy some more.

CARLY. I work at a demanding yet glamorous job. I spend hours at the gym to keep in shape. I enjoy an active night life, taking full advantage of the array of sensual pleasures that are available to an independent woman like myself. I have a healthy zest for living, and if I allowed myself to, I would sweat a lot. I'm not ashamed of it, I just don't have time for it.

TRENT. Buy some more.

CARLY. I don't think a woman should have to buy antiperspirant every day. That's just not right. *(Pause. Trent continues to work out.)* You sweat a lot, don't you?

TRENT. Some.

CARLY. Don't you find it inconvenient?

TRENT. Men are supposed to sweat.

CARLY. All the time?

TRENT. Well, no. Not at work, not in the middle of a very important meeting. That's not a good time to sweat. *(Pause.)*

CARLY. Well, you use an antiperspirant, don't you?

TRENT. Sure.

CARLY. Because you don't smell bad. I don't think I could be your girlfriend if you smelled bad.

TRENT. Of course not.

CARLY. Where is it?

TRENT. What?

CARLY. Your antiperspirant.

TRENT. It's in the bathroom, in the medicine chest. *(She exits the stage, still wearing only one shoe. Trent continues to row, huffing and puffing loudly and making unnecessarily violent faces indicating great strain and exertion. Carly re-enters, carrying a large phallic-shaped can of antiperspirant designed in masculine colors: brown and gray and black.)*

CARLY. Is this it?

TRENT. What?

CARLY. This is your antiperspirant?

TRENT. Yes.

CARLY. Well, I have to say I find this very upsetting.

TRENT. Why?

CARLY. Because yours is so much bigger than mine. I don't

think that's fair.

TRENT. Sorry.

CARLY. I think this is discrimination.

TRENT. I don't know what to tell you.

CARLY. I mean, didn't you just say that men are supposed to sweat?

TRENT. Sometimes.

CARLY. Well, then, if anything, my antiperspirant should be bigger than yours.

TRENT. I'm sweating now.

CARLY. Trent, this is really bothering me.

TRENT. I'm sorry, Carly. I don't know what else to say.

CARLY. This is the kind of discrimination that I run up against every day. You can't possibly understand that. You're not a woman.

TRENT. No, I'm not. I'm sensitive and accommodating, but I'm very much a man.

CARLY. You're allowed to sweat.

TRENT. *(Through gritted teeth.)* And I'm becoming more of a man by the minute.

CARLY. It's not fair.

TRENT. Carly?

CARLY. What.

TRENT. I might need to have sex when I finish working out.

CARLY. *(Bored.)* Oh, all right. *(She puts his antiperspirant on the vanity and slips on the other shoe she's been holding all this time. She checks her face in the mirror, musses her hair a little, then arranges herself in a provocative pose. He pays no attention to her and continues rowing. After a moment, she checks her watch.)* How long is this going to take?

TRENT. At least half an hour.

CARLY. Half an hour!?

TRENT. Yes. I have to spend ten minutes working up to my target heart rate and then twenty minutes maintaining it.

CARLY. But half an hour, that's so ... *long.*

TRENT. Then I have to pump iron for another hour.

CARLY. What?

TRENT. Then I have to cool down.

CARLY. I can't believe this.

TRENT. Well, you want me to have a good body, don't you? You want me to achieve my full potential as a man, don't you?

CARLY. I guess.

TRENT. I'm doing this for you.

CARLY. I know, and I appreciate it, honey.

TRENT. I'm going to get a buzz cut. I'm going to have massive arms and I'm going to get a tattoo. I'm going to wear a white T-shirt and faded blue jeans. I don't want the jeans to be tight, that's too gay. And my ass is good enough to carry off the baggy look. But the T-shirt should be as tight as it possibly can, stretched against my washboard stomach and chiseled pecs, with just the hint of my tattoo showing below the sleeve. I'm going to be so hot that wherever I go people will stare at me and want to fuck me.

CARLY. *(Bored.)* Great.

TRENT. I'm doing this for you.

CARLY. Thanks. *(She rises and crosses to the vanity, listlessly. She notices the pink box her antiperspirant came in, picks it up, and reads the label.)* Why do they make the box so big, then? I mean, if the thing itself is so little.

TRENT. Christ, Carly. Don't you have anything better to think about?

CARLY. I'm sorry. This is important to me. *(She spots something on the label.)* Trent, look! They have an eight hundred number! *(She kicks all the stuff on the floor around, looking for the phone. When she finds it, she drops into the easy chair and dials. Dialing, purposefully.)* One — eight hundred — M-Y-S-T-E-E-K. *(Pause.)* Hey, that's not how you spell it. *(Pause.)* Hello, is this Mystique? This is Carly. How are you? Great. Listen, I have a question. Two questions. First, you know how your phone number is one eight hundred Mystique? Only it's spelled wrong. Well, M-Y-S-T-E-E-K. That's not how you spell it. Oh. Really? *(She checks the keypad of her phone.)* Oh my God, that is so weird. *(Back into receiver.)* You're right! That is so weird. Hey, hold on, okay? *(To Trent.)* Trent, did you know there's not a Q on the keypad of a phone? Can you believe it? I never even knew that. *(Back into receiver.)* That is so wild. Oh, so my other question is: My boyfriend just bought me the Mega Lifestyle size of your Spring Morning Dew scented antiperspirant for Baby Fresh Extra Sensitive Skin? Well, the box is really big, but the actual antiperspirant, the product itself, is quite small. It's embarrassing, actually. I mean, it could be lip gloss. So I just wondered, how can you sell something so small and insignificant in a box that makes it look like there's something really big and important inside? *(Pause.)* Oh, really. Uh-huh. Well, sure. Okay. Thanks. Hey listen, do you like General Foods International Coffee? *(Staring at the phone.)* She hung up. *(She sits, stunned, then crosses to the vanity. She checks her face and tries rearranging her hair, but her heart isn't in it. After a moment, she crosses to Trent, who is still rowing diligently.)* Trent, I don't think that woman was telling me the truth.

TRENT. What woman?

CARLY. That Mystique woman. She said the reason the box was so big was because it created an aura of mystery and expectation, that it was all part of the Mystique mystique. And then she said that the reason the actual product was so small is because it's concentrated so you don't need as much. But then she hung up on me. I mean, she just hung up on me. *(She takes off her spiked heels, grabs the cowboy boots she was wearing earlier, drops into the easy chair and pulls them on. She then gets up and stomps around, preoccupied.)* Trent, I am really upset. I think I am more upset than I have ever been. I feel like I've been cheated! Other people are taking things that belong to me!

TRENT. Go to your aerobics class. Work it off.

CARLY. *(Picking up the Mystique box.)* How can something like this be allowed to happen? I mean, would you just look at the size of this box? What was I supposed to think when I saw that?

TRENT. Buy a new CD. Buy a new CD player.

CARLY. I thought there was something fabulous and special inside! Something that would make my life better! And then, after they intentionally got my hopes up — you heard what she said, this box was specifically designed to create an aura of mystery and expectation — then I open the box and what do I find inside? *(Picks up the antiperspirant container, a little hysterical.)* This! What is this? This is nothing!

TRENT. Go back to school. Change your career.

CARLY. *(Angry.)* Trent! My entire value system has been shot to hell! I don't know what to believe, or who to trust. What am I supposed to do now? *(Trent stops rowing and looks at her.*

TRENT. What am I, your therapist?

CARLY. Well, no.

TRENT. No. I haven't got a clue what you're supposed to do, Carly. And frankly, I think your putting me on the spot like this is a little insensitive. Are you trying to make me feel inadequate?

CARLY. No, of course not.

TRENT. I *know* that the only thing I have going for me is the fact that I look so damn good, okay? So I'm using it. I'm working out, striving to better myself the one way I know how, and you interrupt me with a personal problem that I'm sorry, you should be able to resolve on your own.

CARLY. But —

TRENT. Don't get me wrong, Carly. I'm here for you. I love you. You're a very beautiful woman and you make me feel really important when we're seen together in public. *(Exhausted.)* But I can only give so much. I can't be strong for both of us. You've got be strong for yourself.

CARLY. I know that. I'm very strong.

TRENT. So *be* strong. Take charge. Meet the challenge. Be a person who *acts,* not someone who is acted *upon.* Okay?

CARLY. Okay.

TRENT. All better?

CARLY. All better.

TRENT. Good. Because, don't forget, I want to have sex after I finish working out. *(He resumes rowing. Carly watches him, then crosses to the window with great resolve. She tosses the pink box and the antiperspirant container out the window.)*

CARLY. I don't need Mystique. Because you know what? I'm never going to sweat again. Sweating is for idiots. *(Pause.)*

Look at all those idiots down there. Stupid vacuous people with boring insipid lives. I bet not *one* of them is a person who acts. God. How depressing. So many people and all of them completely unnecessary. *(Pause.)* Trent, I want to show you something. *(She crosses to the vanity and digs through her purse.)* I got this the other day, I meant to show it to you, but I forgot. *(She pulls out a petite handgun.)* Look! Isn't that sweet? It's a Lady Smith & Wesson. Specifically designed for the delicate contours of the feminine hand. Little pearl handle. I love this gun. I *love* it! *(She skips gleefully around the loft, then stops U. of Trent, who continues to row, oblivious to her.)* It makes me feel so *safe. (She raises the gun and points it at his head. A long pause, then she lowers the gun and crosses to the window. She watches the people below for a moment, then casually fires a shot in their direction. Smiling, she looks back at Trent to see if he's paying attention; he isn't, of course. She fires another shot; a scream is heard from below. She is getting giddy. She fires a third shot. Excited.)* Trent! I hit one! *(She fires another shot, wondrously.)* This is fun. *(Trent continues to row. On her fifth shot, the lights blackout.)*

PROPERTY LIST

Make-up (CARLY)
Hair gel (CARLY)
Flashy dangle earrings (CARLY)
Paper bag with box, containing antipersperant (TRENT)
Spike-heeled shoes (CARLY)
Portable rowing machine (TRENT)
Men's deodorant aerosol can (CARLY)
Purse (CARLY)
Small gun (CARLY)

BACHELOR HOLIDAY

BACHELOR HOLIDAY was first produced by Alarm Dog Repertory at HOME for Contemporary Theater and Art (Randy Rolison, Artistic Director), in New York City, on June 14, 1991. It was directed by David Munnell and the stage manager was Tara Buckley. The cast was as follows:

FORD .... Alan Ball
NORRIS .... Marc Ashmore
HUNTER .... David Levine

CHARACTERS

FORD
NORRIS
HUNTER

Three men in their late twenties who share an apartment in New York.

BACHELOR HOLIDAY

A dining room. All that's really necessary is a dinette table and a couple of chairs, preferably of the Jetsons variety, but any kind that suggests a house of deadbeats will do.

Lights come up on Ford folding laundry. After a moment, Norris enters groggily. He stares pointedly at Ford.

FORD. What?
NORRIS. Are you really folding your underwear?
FORD. Yes.
NORRIS. You are a total dick.
FORD. Thank you.
NORRIS. You know, when you stop and think about it, you probably spend about eleven years of your life doing laundry, right? A year and a half of that just folding your underwear. When nobody ever sees it and when you put it on, it never looks wrinkled anyway.
FORD. It's a Zen thing.
NORRIS. I stopped folding my underwear a long time ago. I just wad it up and throw it in a drawer.
FORD. That's really beautiful, Norris. Thank you for sharing.
NORRIS. Yeah, well, I'm going to take that year and a half as vacation sometime, but you're going to be on your deathbed and be saying, where did all the time go?
FORD. Why don't I just kill myself right now to avoid that moment of horrible realization.
NORRIS. It would save time.
FORD. And time is money.
NORRIS. I have to talk to you, this is serious.
FORD. What?

NORRIS. I have to ask you something.
FORD. Okay.
NORRIS. But first you have to promise to tell me the truth.
FORD. Okay, what?
NORRIS. Do you promise?
FORD. What is it?
NORRIS. It's really important.
FORD. What? *(Pause.)*
NORRIS. *(Dead serious)* Did you eat my Cocoa Crispies?
FORD. No.
NORRIS. Liar.
FORD. I didn't.
NORRIS. You know, if you just fold these shirts in half instead of doing this tri-fold thing, then you only have to fold it once this way, and so you've saved two whole steps. Three, if it's a long sleeve shirt.
FORD. *(Staring at him)* Thanks.
NORRIS. You really didn't eat my Cocoa Crispies?
FORD. I don't eat that shit, Norris.
NORRIS. No, you eat bean scum and leaves.
FORD. Right. So why are you even asking me?
NORRIS. Well, I just bought a box day before yesterday, and I've only eaten one bowl's worth, and now it's gone.
FORD. Oh, you know what? I think Hunter used it.
NORRIS. What do you mean he used it?
FORD. As bait for the glue traps.
NORRIS. Are you serious? That is so incredibly insensitive.
FORD. Just make him buy you some more.
NORRIS. Yeah, and he'll buy the smallest size, just like whenever he has to get milk for the house he only gets a quart and I always get a gallon. Besides, that's not the point. The point is that those were *my* Cocoa Crispies —
FORD. Oh, please. I'll go buy you some right now.
NORRIS. Don't take his side, Ford.
FORD. I'm not taking his side, I just don't want to listen to you bitch and moan for the next hour and a half about breakfast cereal. I got up very early this morning, Norris. I watched the sun rise, I meditated, I did my laundry and now

I'm folding it slowly and quietly, allowing the discipline of folding to distract my mind from itself so it can be open to the true nature of things. Because this afternoon, I have an appointment with a prospective client which might mean major bucks for me, and you are upsetting the delicate balance I am striving to achieve in the hopes of attaining that goal.

NORRIS. I'm merely expressing myself.

FORD. Yeah, well express this. *(He flings a pair of underwear at Norris, hitting him in the face.)*

NORRIS. Gross, you dick. I don't want your cheesy old underwear in my face.

FORD. How's your head?

NORRIS. Fine.

FORD. You're not hung over?

NORRIS. I don't get hangovers.

FORD. You've just forgotten what it feels like not to have one.

NORRIS. We did not drink that much.

FORD. Maybe not for Dylan Thomas.

NORRIS. Wimp.

FORD. You guys drank half a bottle of tequila. You were tanked.

NORRIS. Hunter was tanked. I was fine.

FORD. You were both sloppy, smelly, fall-down, talk-too-loud and stick-your-face-too-close-to-mine drunk. And, you were farting indiscriminately.

NORRIS. You're just jealous.

FORD. You pissed in the sink.

NORRIS. *(Horrified)* I did not.

FORD. Oh yes, you did.

NORRIS. I would never.

FORD. See? You blacked out.

NORRIS. You guys always do that and then I get up to brush my teeth in the morning and the sink smells like piss and I just want to blow chunks all over the place. I can't believe I did that. My opinion of myself has just taken a major dive.

FORD. Good. You need a more realistic self image.

NORRIS. Why would I do that?
FORD. Because it's fun.
NORRIS. Fun? Peeing in a sink is fun?
FORD. Sure. Peeing anywhere you're not supposed to pee is fun.
NORRIS. I guess that makes New York fun capitol of the world.
FORD. Oh, come on. Haven't you ever peed off a building?
NORRIS. They have special phone lines for that, Ford.
FORD. If you hadn't been so drunk, you'd remember how much fun it was.
NORRIS. You know what's really fun? Peeing in a toaster. Only make sure it's turned on first. What time is it?
FORD. Eight thirty. Eleven. I don't know. Shit. Now I'm totally unmotivated.
NORRIS. Don't think of it as unmotivated. Think of it as relaxed.
FORD. If you relax too much, you die.
NORRIS. Hey, Zen boy. Listen to yourself. See, you keep thinking that motivation is something you need. When, in reality, it just gets in your way.
FORD. I am so weird. I am. I felt really great when I got up this morning, full of energy, and optimism about the day ahead, and now, all of a sudden, I'm on the verge of a coma.
NORRIS. Go back to sleep.
FORD. No.
NORRIS. Why not?
FORD. Because then my energy will be all fucked up for my interview and I won't get the job and then I won't be able to buy that Missoni suit. No, I should just stop thinking about it and do it.
NORRIS. Do what?
FORD. Well ... I should go over my portfolio, make sure it's in order. I should shave. I should go to the gym. I should write about a million letters to all the people I ever knew in my life, I should go back to school and get my degree, I should rid myself of all negative thinking. I should take an active part in local government, I should make a personal

commitment to a healthier environment, I should be the catalyst for my dysfunctional family to begin healing.

NORRIS. Oh, lighten up. Look at what you've accomplished already. Look at all those perfect little underwears in a stack.

FORD. Presentation is everything.

NORRIS. You should work at the Gap.

FORD. Now what?

NORRIS. Drink some coffee.

FORD. Maybe I've got chronic fatigue syndrome.

NORRIS. Maybe you're just a whining yuppie.

FORD. *(Stung.)* I am not a yuppie.

NORRIS. You shave on a regular basis. You refer to people as clients. And — look me in the eye and tell me this isn't true — whenever you get depressed, you buy something you don't need and then you feel better immediately.

FORD. Yeah, but I have not worn a pair of suspenders since I was in *Godspell* in high school.

NORRIS. You have a gold card.

FORD. I am not a yuppie.

NORRIS. Let's take a simple quiz. Which of the following do you have: Doctor?

FORD. Well, yeah.

NORRIS. Dentist?

FORD. Sure.

NORRIS. Accountant?

FORD. Of course.

NORRIS. Shrink?

FORD. You know I do.

NORRIS. Hairdresser?

FORD. Yeah, but I haven't been real happy with her lately.

NORRIS. Acupuncturist? *(Pause.)*

FORD. Is there a point to all this?

NORRIS. You have a *staff.*

FORD. Oh, please. I am a functioning member of a service economy. I buy services that I really need from professionals who do a really good job.

NORRIS. You are a total sucker for new and embarrassing ways to spend money.

FORD. Okay, but part of that is that I'm a Taurus, right, and I have this psychic need for material comfort.
NORRIS. Oh, that's convenient. Yuppie.
FORD. No way am I a yuppie.
NORRIS. The only way you're not a yuppie is if I never peed in the sink.
FORD. Deal.
NORRIS. Wow. I guess reality is not nearly as confining as I thought.
FORD. Do you have any dope? *(Hunter enters. He is large and loud.)*
HUNTER. Anybody know anybody who wants to stay up all night for ten bucks an hour?
NORRIS. Doing what?
HUNTER. Watching equipment.
NORRIS. What kind of equipment?
HUNTER. Two 12-foot scaffolding towers. A bunch of cable.
NORRIS. Cash?
HUNTER. I think so, I'm pretty sure.
FORD. Do it, Norris. You could pee off the top and nobody would ever know.
NORRIS. Why do they need to be watched?
HUNTER. Keep people from stealing them, basically. Trashing them. Sleeping on them, I don't know. You interested?
NORRIS. Maybe.
HUNTER. Well, I gotta know now, because they have to be watched tonight.
NORRIS. From when to when?
HUNTER. About two a.m. to seven tomorrow morning.
NORRIS. That's only five hours.
HUNTER. Yeah, something like that.
NORRIS. Well, that's only fifty dollars.
HUNTER. Do you want to do it or not?
NORRIS. Stay up all night for just fifty bucks.
HUNTER. It's not like you have to work or anything, just sit on your fat ass all night long.
NORRIS. Yeah, and make myself available to any stray psycho killer who just happens to wander into the picture.

HUNTER. Forget it.
NORRIS. Where.
HUNTER. Village. NYU.
NORRIS. I'll do it for a hundred.
HUNTER. Norris. The offer is ten bucks an hour. We can't afford any more. I'm pouring a shitload of my own money into this thing already, because I need it for my reel.
NORRIS. Seventy five.
HUNTER. Ten bucks, Norris. Ten bucks an hour. There is no room for discussion. Do you want to do it or not, because there are other people who will. You know you're always bitching about how you don't have any money, I just thought you might want to, but if you don't, forget it. I don't care. *(Pause.)*
NORRIS. Yeah, I'll do it. Tonight?
HUNTER. Tonight.
NORRIS. Shit, it's supposed to rain, isn't it? Perfect. This always happens to me.
HUNTER. What's for breakfast?
NORRIS. Not Cocoa Crispies, thanks to you.
HUNTER. What?
NORRIS. Ford says you used my Cocoa Crispies for the glue traps.
FORD. I said I thought, I didn't say I knew for sure.
HUNTER. I used whatever was there, I don't know what it was.
NORRIS. Well, you owe me a box. And a big box, not one of those little ones. It was the biggest one.
HUNTER. I'm really hungry.
FORD. I have some food in the fridge, you're welcome to it.
HUNTER. Is it real?
FORD. I've been operating under the assumption that it is, and I haven't run into any trouble.
NORRIS. Yet.
HUNTER. Because some of that stuff you eat, Ford, I don't know. It's almost like food, but it doesn't quite make it. And I can only eat real food.

FORD. Well, there's tofu — *(Norris makes a game show "wrong" buzzer sound.)*
HUNTER. Not real. Not even close. I need something from the four major food groups.
FORD. Tofu is protein. Wait, no — it's a vegetable.
HUNTER. The four major food groups, Ford. Sugar, salt, grease and alcohol.
FORD. You are twisted.
HUNTER. Mars bar and a beer, it's a complete meal. What else do you have?
FORD. Tabouli — *(Norris makes a game show "wrong" buzzer sound.)*
HUNTER. Give me something I can work with, babe.
FORD. A kumquat — *(Norris and Hunter stare at each other.)*
HUNTER. What the fuck is that?
FORD. And some cheese.
HUNTER. Cheese I can deal with. Thanks, Binky. *(He exits.)*
NORRIS. I'll never see those Cocoa Crispies again. You know I never will.
FORD. Norris, if you love something, set it free.
NORRIS. Thank you, Swami Bessie. I'm serious, though. Did you notice how he just kind of shrugged it off, when I said you owe me a box and he just said, "I'm really hungry." I don't know why I should expect anything different. He does the same thing all the time, always has. Do you know how long I have known him? He just acts like he owns the fucking world —
FORD. I'm going across the street. Do you want anything?
NORRIS. What are you getting?
FORD. Coffee.
NORRIS. Would you get me some?
FORD. Sure.
NORRIS. My money's upstairs.
FORD. Don't worry about it. *(He exits. Norris examines Ford's laundry, begins re-folding it. Hunter enters carrying a plastic bowl.)*
HUNTER. Look at this cheese. Is that weird or what?
NORRIS. It's just cheese.
HUNTER. What kind, though.

NORRIS. I don't know. Healthy.

HUNTER. Fuck. We need to get a roommate who eats like a real person. Didn't we used to have some donuts?

NORRIS. Yeah, about a month ago.

HUNTER. So, you'll do this, you'll watch that shit tonight?

NORRIS. I said I would.

HUNTER. Okay, I'm calling Bart, so you can't wimp out when it gets to be about midnight and say, oh shit, I don't feel so good. Maybe I should stay at home.

NORRIS. I would never.

HUNTER. Right.

NORRIS. You might find this hard to believe, Hunter, but some people around here stick to it when they give you their word. Just like some people around here have respect for other people's private property.

HUNTER. Oh fuck, now what?

NORRIS. It's not the Cocoa Crispies themselves, Hunter, it's the principle of the thing —

HUNTER. Norris, there was only about half a — there was only about a spoonful in there. I had to put something on the glue trap as bait, what do you want me to do? Go buy a whole thing of cereal just to use about a spoonful? You're the one who's so freaked out by the mice, anyway.

NORRIS. I'm not freaked out by them, I just hate going into the pantry and having to dig through rat turds to get anything to eat.

HUNTER. If you weren't allergic to cats we wouldn't have this problem —

NORRIS. Oh, now I'm supposed to feel guilty because I'm a human being?

HUNTER. Who said you were supposed to feel guilty about anything?

NORRIS. What makes you think mice are going to like Cocoa Crispies anyway?

HUNTER. Are you kidding? Mice eat anything. They even eat those rice cake things that Ford eats, they're always getting into those.

NORRIS. So how come you didn't use those for bait? How

come it's always my shit that you take?

HUNTER. Well, I figured this was going to be the last thing that some poor mouse would ever eat, I should give it a break. Those rice wads taste like styrofoam. At least Cocoa Crispies has flavor.

NORRIS. Ah-hah! See?

HUNTER. What?

NORRIS. You said that Cocoa Crispies has flavor, which means that you know what they taste like, which means you ate some.

HUNTER. Well, yeah. In my life I have eaten Cocoa Crispies.

NORRIS. In the last twenty-four *hours,* you have eaten *my* Cocoa Crispies.

HUNTER. You know, I could understand this if it was your stereo, or your computer, or your car —

NORRIS. I don't have any of those things.

HUNTER. So, what, you're making up for it, being like car-proud, with your fucking cereal? Is that it? Are you Cocoa *Crispie*-proud?

NORRIS. All I want you to do is to admit that you took my cereal without asking, for you to apologize, and for you to buy me some more.

HUNTER. See, you shouldn't have done that. If I know that's what you want me to do, then automatically, I don't want to do it. It's just a basic response I have. Sorry.

NORRIS. That's like saying, oh, I'm so sorry I just shot you in the face, but I've always been a psycho killer, so it wasn't really my fault.

HUNTER. Works for me.

NORRIS. There is no talking to you.

HUNTER. I guess not, so why don't you shut up? *(Ford enters, carrying a bag of groceries.)* What'd you get?

FORD. Lots of good stuff. I got plain yogurt —

HUNTER. Blech.

FORD. Some skim milk —

HUNTER. That shit is paint, man.

FORD. Some real milk, for you two fat-suckers —

NORRIS. See, he gets a whole gallon.
FORD. And — the largest box of Cocoa Crispies ever in the history of God.
HUNTER. Whoa! Excellent.
NORRIS. This doesn't mean you still don't owe me a box.
FORD. And three cups of coffee.
HUNTER. You're all right, man.
NORRIS. Oh, sure, somebody gives you shit, they're all right. *(He turns to leave.)*
FORD. Where are you going?
NORRIS. I'm going to get some coffee cups.
FORD. They're in cups already.
NORRIS. Yeah, but coffee tastes better when it's in a ceramic cup.
HUNTER. Do you have any scientific data to back that up?
NORRIS. *Yes. (He exits.)*
HUNTER. He's fucking out of control, Ford.
FORD. I know. Yesterday he yelled at me because I rinsed something off too much before I put it in the dishwasher.
HUNTER. I may have to resort to violence.
FORD. He's just frustrated.
HUNTER. Well, so am I, but I'm not an asshole about it. *(Ford gives him a look.)* Okay, but when I'm an asshole, it doesn't bother me nearly as much as when *he's* one. What is he so frustrated by, anyway?
FORD. His life. What are you so frustrated by?
HUNTER. His life. *(A slightly awkward pause.)* Ugh, look, there's a bee in this bowl. On this cheese. *(Another pause, as they stare at it.)*
FORD. Bees are so cool. Look how they're designed.
HUNTER. It looks stoned.
FORD. It's eating that cheese.
HUNTER. Bees don't eat cheese.
FORD. That one does.
HUNTER. I came in the kitchen the other day, there was a goddamn bumble bee scratching its back on the light bulb. Just kind of flying around, rubbing its back up against the light bulb. Can you believe it? Bugs in this house are so

weird. I mean, if you're going to be nature, act natural.
FORD. It's goat cheese.
HUNTER. What is this, bees eating cheese, scratching their backs? Man, this sucks.
FORD. Hey, bees have a hard life. I mean, they work all the time. *(Pause.)*
HUNTER. So, Binky. I have a new girlfriend.
FORD. I know, I met her.
HUNTER. No. That one's history.
FORD. The blonde?
HUNTER. Yeah.
FORD. I liked her.
HUNTER. You can have her.
FORD. What? She was nice, she was smart, she was pretty —
HUNTER. She was pathological.
FORD. How was she pathological?
HUNTER. Total tease.
FORD. Really.
HUNTER. I mean, she played some major, major games.
FORD. That's too bad.
HUNTER. She's totally afraid of commitment. I mean, I was there. I was ready. *(Pause.)*
FORD. And she wasn't.
HUNTER. No way. She said she was, but when it came down to it, she chickened out.
FORD. How long did you guys see each other?
HUNTER. Long enough. A month.
FORD. Wow.
HUNTER. You can tell pretty much everything about somebody after a month, don't you think?
FORD. It's a long time.
HUNTER. This new girl, though, she's pretty cool. You would like her.
FORD. Great. What's her name?
HUNTER. Linda.
FORD. What does she do?
HUNTER. She's an artist.
FORD. Cool. What kind of art?

HUNTER. You know. Neurotic woman art.
FORD. Like what?
HUNTER. Mostly video stuff, I think. I've only seen one thing. She's lying in this bathtub and then all this animated shit comes out of her head.
FORD. She makes films?
HUNTER. No way, she's just some kind of artist. Something bogus. Like performance art. *(Pause.)*
FORD. Do you like her?
HUNTER. I don't know. I might. I do sometimes.
FORD. You guys must have a lot in common. You know, with her making videos.
HUNTER. Some. She's kind of a Jap, though. She has a car.
FORD. Great.
HUNTER. A Miata. *(Norris enters carrying a tray; on it are three coffee mugs, three spoons, a half-empty pint container of ice cream and an opened can of chocolate syrup.)*
NORRIS. You guys. I was looking on the calendar on front of the fridge and guess what today is.
HUNTER. Your birthday.
NORRIS. No. Guess.
FORD. I give up, what?
NORRIS. The anniversary of the first atomic bomb.
HUNTER. Excellent.
NORRIS. Don't you think that's weird, they would choose that date to commemorate? And with an illustration, no less.
FORD. Let's celebrate.
HUNTER. Could this be a tequila-related event?
FORD. Not for me.
NORRIS. *(Indicating tray.)* No, that's what all this is for, to celebrate.
HUNTER. *(To Ford.)* Aw, Binky. You never join our reindeer games.
FORD. I have a job interview today, I can't.
NORRIS. Let's just have some ice cream and coffee.
HUNTER. I don't know. It seems so wimpy.
NORRIS. It's ten o'clock in the morning, Hunter. I can't

start this early.

HUNTER. Man, you are turning into an old man. An old man with no balls. An old man with no dick.

NORRIS. Noon.

HUNTER. Start whenever you want, I'm starting now. *(He exits.)*

NORRIS. Great. Now he's going to make me spend my whole day off drunk.

FORD. I thought you didn't get drunk.

NORRIS. I don't get hangovers. I get drunk. A lot. A little too much, know what I mean?

FORD. Just say no.

NORRIS. Yeah, but then he'll say I'm wimping out.

FORD. So?

NORRIS. I just don't want him to think that. He already thinks he's such a giant among men, I can't let him get away with it.

FORD. That's a really stupid reason, Norris.

NORRIS. Yeah, well, he doesn't ride you like he rides me.

FORD. Only because you let him.

NORRIS. I do not let him. I do not. I am the only one around here who calls him on his shit.

FORD. You antagonize him, which just makes him antagonize you more.

NORRIS. So what, I'm just supposed to let him get away with everything?

FORD. Of course not, not if he's seriously infringing upon your rights as a human being. But every little thing, God, it gets so exhausting —

NORRIS. Him eating my Cocoa Crispies *is* an infringement on my rights.

FORD. I guess it's just a question of perspective.

NORRIS. Don't you think I have a right to have food in this house without people eating it?

FORD. Of course.

NORRIS. I mean, I'm sorry. I just think if something's important to you, you should speak up about it.

FORD. You just like to argue.

NORRIS. What's wrong with that?

FORD. *Nothing.*

NORRIS. Then why are you making such a big deal about it?

FORD. I'm not making a big deal. *You* were the one who sounded a little concerned about how much you were drinking, earlier. I think you're letting this competition thing with Hunter turn into the perfect excuse for you to drink *more* —

NORRIS. *(An edge.)* I don't need an excuse, Ford, and I don't need a shrink either, okay? *(Pause.)*

FORD. Okay. Sorry.

NORRIS. You want ice cream in your coffee?

FORD. No.

NORRIS. What? It's good.

FORD. No thanks.

NORRIS. Aren't you going to put yours in a cup?

FORD. No.

NORRIS. Here, pour the milk in first, then pour the coffee in, it tastes better that way. *(He pours milk into a mug, then reaches for Ford's paper cup of coffee.)*

FORD. Norris, don't —

NORRIS. It's good.

FORD. I mean it. *(He takes the coffee from Norris.)* Look ... even if that was going to be the best cup of coffee I had ever had in my life, and even if drinking it out of this paper cup is going to make it the most rancid cup ever, since the beginning of time, I would rather drink it out of this paper cup. Can you understand that?

NORRIS. You're serious, aren't you?

FORD. Yes. You have got to stop telling me how to change everything I do so that I do everything like you, okay? I'm not you, Norris, we're two different people. We have two different ways of doing things. And they're both valid.

NORRIS. I only tell you things because I think they'll help you.

FORD. I appreciate that, but you would really help me out if you quit doing it altogether.

NORRIS. Okay. God.

FORD. Thank you. *(Hunter enters holding a bottle of tequila in one hand and a glue trap with a mouse caught in it in the other.*

HUNTER. Hey, Norris, those Cocoa Crispies did the trick. Look what I found.

NORRIS. Oh, gross.

FORD. Is it still alive?

HUNTER. Yeah. *(Pause.)*

NORRIS. Throw it away.

FORD. No, don't.

NORRIS. You want to keep it?

FORD. You can't just throw it away, and let it lay there in the garbage and die a slow and agonizing death.

NORRIS. It's a mouse.

FORD. That doesn't mean it can't suffer.

HUNTER. Eat it. It's lower on the food chain.

NORRIS. *You're* lower on the food chain.

HUNTER. Eat me, then.

FORD. We have to do something.

NORRIS. What, you want to pry it loose and set it free? We can't have mice in the house, Ford. They're filthy, they eat our food, they carry disease —

FORD. I know that. But now that we've caught it, we have a responsibility, we can't just let it lay there and die. We have to kill it.

HUNTER. Yeah!

NORRIS. You don't want us to let it die, so you want to kill it. That makes a lot of sense.

HUNTER. Geek it!

FORD. We have to put it out of its misery. We have to alleviate its suffering.

HUNTER. Drown it.

FORD. That's a terrible way to die.

NORRIS. Oh, well, let's get it some morphine, call in a priest, hold its little mouse hand and say, "Go toward the light."

FORD. Something fast.

HUNTER. Put it in the blender. Put it in one of those splarby health drinks you make, I'm sure it's got lots of protein.

NORRIS. Alleviate its suffering, get serious. You sound like *L.A. Law.*

FORD. Look at it, Norris. Look at its eyes. You don't think it's suffering?

NORRIS. What are you, the prince of mice? Next thing you know you'll get rid of all the bug spray in the house because it makes the roaches suffer.

FORD. Actually, that wouldn't be a bad idea —

NORRIS. You have lost it, Ford. All this new age shit has scrambled your brain.

FORD. Not because of the roaches suffering, I don't care about that, but because that shit's poison, man. *That's* the kind of stuff that's fucking up your allergies.

NORRIS. Wait a minute. You don't care about the roaches, but here you are all concerned about this mouse? What's the difference? *(Pause.)*

FORD. When I look at this mouse, I see it suffering. I don't see roaches suffering.

NORRIS. When bums come up to us on the street, you're always saying don't give them money —

HUNTER. You don't have any money to give them anyway.

NORRIS. Fuck off. You're always saying don't give them money because you're interfering with their karma when you do. And they're suffering.

FORD. Yeah, but I am not personally responsible for them being where they are. We are responsible for this mouse being in this glue trap. It is suffering because of us. The least we can do, the most humane thing we can do, is to end its suffering.

NORRIS. By killing it.

FORD. Yes.

NORRIS. That is the stupidest argument I have ever heard.

FORD. You think by throwing it in the garbage, we're not killing it?

HUNTER. I think we should see how many different ways we can make it suffer. Put toothpicks in it, pour Drano on it, put it in the microwave —

NORRIS. I will not have that mouse in the microwave.

HUNTER. The glue trap's made out of Styrofoam, it's microwave safe.
FORD. Were you a Nazi in a former life?
HUNTER. I hope so.
FORD. Here, give it to me. *(He takes the glue trap.)* Shit, poor thing. Sorry, bud, you were just in the wrong place at the wrong time. *(He turns and exits. Norris follows him off. Hunter remains on stage, eating cereal.)*
NORRIS. Where are you going?
FORD. I'm going to get a plastic bag.
NORRIS. Don't tell me you're going to suffocate it.
FORD. No, I am not going to suffocate him, that's a terrible way to die. I'm going to put him in a plastic bag, and then I am going to put that in a paper bag, and then —
NORRIS. How do you know it's a him?
FORD. Her, then. It.
NORRIS. I mean, if you're going to be all ethically correct, you can't afford to let a little sexism creep in —
FORD. And then I am going to put this mouse of whatever sex, neither of which is superior or inferior but rather complimentary, mirroring the other in a beautiful cosmic harmony, are you satisfied? Now I am putting it into this paper bag —
NORRIS. Why? *(Pause.)*
FORD. Because ... that way it way it won't be able to see when I bash its brains in with this hammer. *(He enters, holding a folded over paper bag and a hammer. Norris is right behind him.)*
NORRIS. You mean that way *you* won't have to look at it when you bash its brains in with that hammer.
FORD. That too.
HUNTER. Binky the Terminator!
NORRIS. I think if you're going to kill it, you should have to watch it die.
FORD. I am so glad you feel compelled to share with me your way of executing mice, Norris. Do you see what you're doing? This is exactly what I was talking about earlier. Besides, that is a totally vegetarian argument, and you eat *Vienna sausages.*

HUNTER. Now, those I did not touch. *(Ford sets the bag on the table and steps back. Pause.)*
FORD. Should we say a prayer or something?
NORRIS. You should pray nobody ever finds out what a dink you are.
FORD. I'm sorry I have to kill you, mouse.
HUNTER. *(Mouse voice.)* Not half as sorry as I am. *(Ford laughs in spite of himself.)* Do it, Binky!
NORRIS. What are you waiting for? *(Ford hits the bag with the hammer, hard. He hits it several times, probably a bit more than necessary. Pause.)*
FORD. I really need to get laid.
NORRIS. This is so lame.
HUNTER. How do you feel? Did you get a boner?
NORRIS. I just watched a grown man savagely murder a defenseless animal, all because it was the humane thing to do. I live with this person. I share a bathroom with this person. I —
HUNTER. What's that on your leg?
NORRIS. Where?
HUNTER. There.
NORRIS. Ugh! Some of that mouse's guts splarbed out of that bag onto my leg! Ugh! *(He does a little dance of revulsion and runs out of the room.)*
FORD. I'm exhausted.
HUNTER. Don't you want to look at it?
FORD. No!
HUNTER. Oh, come on. You know you do.
FORD. No.
HUNTER. You have to. *(A pause, then Ford opens the bag. They peer inside.)* Boy, you obliterated that thing.
FORD. You think it's dead?
HUNTER. Dead? It's strawberry yogurt!
FORD. I think I'm going to cry.
HUNTER. Don't wimp out on me, Binky. And whatever you do ... don't think about this poor mouse's wife and six baby kids, waiting back at home for this guy to bring them their dinner.

FORD. Shut up.

HUNTER. Little Timmy Mouse, and Becky Mouse ...

FORD. Shut up!

HUNTER. Their cute little baby mouse faces all scrunched up, saying, "Where's our Daddy?"

FORD. We should write a letter. Dear Mrs. Mouse, we regret to inform you your husband was tragically killed in the line of duty. Here's his body in a bag. We're really sorry. Now, fuck off.

HUNTER. He died big, man.

FORD. I just remembered, I read in the *Science Times,* I think, mice are the only species that really do mate for life, that are completely monogamous.

HUNTER. You must feel really bad now. His poor wife will never get laid again.

FORD. I wonder if mice can feel grief.

HUNTER. I wonder if mice can feel pissed.

FORD. Wow.

HUNTER. What?

FORD. I just killed something. I am the dark angel of death.

HUNTER. Now don't go getting a swelled head.

FORD. I wonder what this does for me karma-wise.

HUNTER. You're fucked. Give it up. Do a shot. *(He has poured shots; he places one in front of Ford.)*

FORD. Oh, man, I really shouldn't. *(Pause.)* What the fuck. *(Norris enters, toweling dry his leg, as Ford and Hunter drink.)*

NORRIS. I cannot believe you got mouse guts on my leg. I will never forgive you. Oh, great. Look at you, Mr. Just Say No.

FORD. Hey. I've been through a lot today.

NORRIS. Spare me.

FORD. God. Can you imagine? I mean, what if you were stuck to this thing, you couldn't move, you couldn't get loose, and then this big — monster, hideous, huge monster thing, picks you up and sticks its big scary face in yours, and starts carrying you around. I wonder how long it was there before we found it.

HUNTER. Who knows? Maybe all night.

FORD. That is so awful. Being trapped. Just waiting. Not really knowing what you're waiting for, but totally powerless. All this time to just — fear. It must have seemed like eternity.
NORRIS. That's the thing about dying, it takes so long.
HUNTER. What the fuck are you talking about?
NORRIS. We're all dying. Right now.
HUNTER. *You* are.
NORRIS. From the minute you're born, you're dying. Life is a complete and total rip-off.
FORD. Speak for yourself.
NORRIS. You just don't want to face up to it because you know you're going to come back as a rat and get your head caved in by some human.
HUNTER. *You're* going to come back as one of us, and have to live with yourself.
FORD. Norris, that's really a simplistic view of karma. It's not so cut and dried, it's not just, "Twenty years ago I stole a nickel, hey, where's that nickel I just had?"
NORRIS. What is it, then, oh master?
FORD. Well, it's not so totally personal. I mean it *is*, but it's ... it's more of a manifestation of the interdependence of all things, and all times. It's like if you have a particular karma issue in this life, it *might* be inherited from a past life, but it also might be from something you're going to do in a future life, and it might be group karma, it might be from somebody else's life altogether.
HUNTER. You mean the reason I'm not rich and famous is because somebody else fucked up?
FORD. Uhm, possibly, sort of.
HUNTER. Well, who? I have a few things to say to him.
FORD. See, all planes, all times, everything exists simultaneously. There's just this one moment, and everything is contained in it. Pyramids being built, the Crusades, the Beatles playing on Ed Sullivan, you taking a whiz in the bathroom sink. It all happens at the same time. That's why there's really no such thing as death.
HUNTER. *(Holding up the mouse bag.)* Tell that to this mouse.

FORD. It's true.

NORRIS. How do *you* know? *(Pause.)*

FORD. I just know it.

NORRIS. What, it came to you in a vision?

FORD. Well, no, but I've read a lot about it, and —

NORRIS. In other words, you read it in a book, so you know it must be true.

FORD. Not exactly.

NORRIS. Yes, exactly. You really have no more idea than the rest of us.

FORD. It's something that I believe.

NORRIS. Just like I believe coffee tastes better when you drink it out of a ceramic cup.

FORD. I think it's a little deeper than that.

NORRIS. How? You are always so morally superior, when the truth is —

FORD. *(Stung.)* I am not morally superior.

NORRIS. — when the truth is you're just as much of a deadbeat lowlife scum as anybody else.

FORD. I never said I wasn't!

NORRIS. You do just as much bullshit for the system, you kiss just as much ass, you're just as shallow and greedy and materialistic as any other American. You can meditate, chant, and burn incense all you want, you can pay some asshole to jab needles into your face and another one to analyze every single little thing that ever happened in your life, but when is the last time you gave your lunch to somebody who was starving? When is the last time you gave your room to some homeless person? When is the last time you gave that fucking designer shirt off your back to somebody who really needed it? *(Pause.)*

FORD. Are you, like, mad at me about something?

NORRIS. *(Shrugs.)* No.

FORD. Really?

NORRIS. No.

FORD. Because if you are, let's talk about it.

NORRIS. Are you guys going to do another shot?

HUNTER. Are you?

NORRIS. Yeah.
HUNTER. Binky?
FORD. No. I can't.
HUNTER. Who's stopping you?
FORD. I have a job interview.
HUNTER. Reschedule it. *(Pause.)*
FORD. Okay.
NORRIS. Wow. Twist your arm.
FORD. Well, what if I get all dressed up and go into the city and then this guy doesn't want to hire me? What if I just lose control and kill him? It's already happened once today.
HUNTER. Really. Killing's like sex. Once you get a taste of it, you just want more.
FORD. I'm only doing the humane thing by staying home.
NORRIS. You are so full of shit.
FORD. Yeah, but Norris? It's *natural* shit. *(He starts putting stacks of laundry into his laundry basket.)* Who refolded my laundry? *(Pause.)*
NORRIS. I just did that one shirt.
FORD. Why?
NORRIS. I don't know. I'll fold it back if you want.
FORD. No, that's not necessary. You just — you are so weird, Norris. *(He exits with laundry basket.)*
NORRIS. Oh, and you're not?
HUNTER. Where are you going?
FORD. *(Off.)* To get my phone.
HUNTER. Okay. But don't even *think* about going to work. *(He pours a shot and places one in front of Norris.)*
NORRIS. Shit. *(Pause.)* Where's yours?
HUNTER. Ford and I already had one. You have to catch up.
NORRIS. Oh, God.
HUNTER. God can't help you now. This is your karma.
NORRIS. Yeah, from somebody else's life. Yours.
HUNTER. Pay the piper, dude. *(Norris drinks the shot and makes a terrible face.)*
NORRIS. Oh God, oh God, oh God. My guts are burning. I'm going to die. I hope you're happy.

HUNTER. Delirious.

NORRIS. Let's do another one. *(Ford enters with a remote phone. Hunter pours three shots.)*

FORD. *(Into phone.)* Yeah, Stuart Shapiro, please. Ford Thompson. Thanks. *(To Hunter.)* Only half that much for me. *(Back into phone.)* Stuart, hi. Listen, I've run into a little snag, I just finished this big job for another client of mine, it's already closed and shipped, but now they have some last minute changes, I'm serious, we had to literally stop the presses. Oh, it's a mess. But I was wondering if we could reschedule for tomorrow. You don't mind? Great. I really hate to call you at the last minute, but I want to take care of this myself, instead of just letting the printer handle it. They'd probably do fine, but just in case. Everybody's put so much work into it, I want to make sure it gets done right. Well, yeah. It's my job. Okay, listen, thanks for being flexible. What's good for you? Ten o'clock it is. Great. Thanks again. *(He switches off the phone.)*

HUNTER. That wasn't so hard, now was it?

FORD. Nope. Plus, now he knows I'm a go-the-extra-mile, get-the-job-done-right kind of guy, no matter how long it takes.

NORRIS. But you're not.

FORD. I am sort of.

NORRIS. You hate to work.

FORD. I hate to work any more than is absolutely necessary. There's a difference. Okay, let's do it.

NORRIS. What do we drink to?

HUNTER. The bomb.

FORD. The bomb.

NORRIS. The bomb. *(They drink.)* Shit.

HUNTER. Think we'll ever see one?

FORD. What?

HUNTER. Nuclear bomb.

FORD. I doubt it.

NORRIS. Oh, I don't know. Some terrorist group will probably get hold of one and blow up a city.

FORD. Do you remember when you first realized, when you were a kid, that they could blow up the whole world?

HUNTER. Yeah.

NORRIS. No.

FORD. I had nightmares about that all the time.

HUNTER. I tied my little brother's G.I. Joe to a Coke bottle full of gasoline and blew it up, and told him he'd been nuked.

NORRIS. Nice. What does your little brother do now?

HUNTER. He works for the I.R.S.

NORRIS. Well, he's obviously paying for your bad karma. I hope you're happy.

FORD. What happened to the G.I. Joe?

HUNTER. He was wasted. His skin melted, you could see all the wires and shit inside him. There was this little box, too, that talked, because he was the talking kind, you'd pull his dog tag and he'd say, "G.I. Joe, reporting for duty sir!" That still worked, actually.

FORD. See? There is no death.

HUNTER. I bet that's why the Japanese are so rich, now.

NORRIS. What?

HUNTER. Well, because they got all the good karma from being blown up by us. We spent all our karma on the bomb.

NORRIS. So why is Germany so rich, then? They killed a bazillion people.

FORD. You guys are so off base. I'm telling you, it's all connected. We're all connected.

NORRIS & HUNTER. *(Singing.)* New York Te-le-phone.

FORD. Fuck you.

HUNTER. Another round, gentlemen?

NORRIS. Oh, why the hell not.

FORD. Not for me.

HUNTER. Binky, you already called in sick.

FORD. Yeah, but I cannot drink tequila all day. I'm too old.

HUNTER. Where are you going?

FORD. Across the street, to spend my karma on a six-pack of beer.

HUNTER. What kind?

FORD. I don't know. Corona.

NORRIS. Yuppie beer.

FORD. Meisterbrau, then. Care to contribute?
NORRIS. I don't have any karma to spare, man.
FORD. I understand.
HUNTER. Would you get me a Mars bar? I need one for my balanced breakfast.
NORRIS. What time is it?
HUNTER. Eleven.
NORRIS. Great. Just in time for *Three's Company.*
HUNTER. All right. What do we do with this mouse? *(Pause.)*
FORD. Throw it away. *(He tosses it in the trash. Norris eyes him.)* What?
NORRIS. I'm not saying a word.
FORD. For once. Be right back. *(He exits.)*
HUNTER. I call the Barco-Lounger.
NORRIS. No way. You had it last night.
HUNTER. You snooze, you lose.
NORRIS. I call the remote, then.
HUNTER. No way, you'll make us watch PBS.
NORRIS. It's good.
HUNTER. It sucks. What's wrong with *Three's Company?*
NORRIS. We gotta get cable.
HUNTER. Just another bill you can't pay. *(They exit.)*
NORRIS. *(Off.)* If we had cable, we'd be able to see stupid teenage sex comedies with real tits instead of a poor excuse like *Three's Company.*
HUNTER. *(Off.)* If we had cable, before you know it we'd have a cleaning person, and then we'd have to get real furniture for them to keep clean, and then somebody would have to get a fax machine, then we'd all have to get real jobs, go to networking parties, get ulcers, high blood pressure, have to stop eating salt, date women who are smarter than we are, invest in socially irresponsible profit-making schemes, get married, get fat, lose our hair, and explode. It's not worth it.
NORRIS. *(Off.)* I still want it.

BLACKOUT

PROPERTY LIST

Basket of clean laundry (FORD) with:
- shirts
- underwear

Plastic bowl (HUNTER)

Bag of groceries (FORD) with:
- yogurt (plain)
- skim milk
- gallon of whole milk
- large box of Cocoa Crispies

Tray (NORRIS) with:
- 3 ceramic coffee mugs
- 3 spoons
- half empty pint container of ice cream
- can of chocolate syrup, opened

Bottle of tequilla (HUNTER)

Glue trap with mouse (HUNTER)

Folded paper bag (FORD)

Hammer (FORD)

3 shot glasses (HUNTER)

Towel (NORRIS)

Remote telephone (FORD)

POWER LUNCH

POWER LUNCH was first produced by Alarm Dog Repertory at the West Bank Cafe Downstairs Theater Bar (Rand Foerster, Artistic Director), in New York City, on July 5, 1989. It was directed by Jeff Mousseau. The cast was as follows:

WOMAN .... Carol McCann
MAN .... Alan Ball
WAITER .... Andrew Watts
WAITRESS .... Carol Halstead

POWER LUNCH was subsequently produced by Alarm Dog Repertory at HOME for Contemporary Theater and Art (Randy Rolison, Artistic Director), in New York City, on November 29, 1991. It was directed by Jeff Mousseau; the set design was by Marc Ashmore; the lighting design was by Richie Williamson and the stage manager was Ellyn Moran. The cast was as follows:

WOMAN .... Carol McCann
MAN .... Alan Ball
WAITER .... Andrew Watts
WAITRESS .... Carol Halstead

CHARACTERS

WOMAN
MAN
WAITER
WAITRESS

POWER LUNCH

Two tables. A Woman in a business suit enters carrying a briefcase. She sits at one table, then opens the briefcase, retrieves a paperback romance novel from inside and begins reading it. There are two empty chairs at her table. After a moment, a Man in a business enters carrying his briefcase. As he approaches the empty table, his briefcase pops open, spilling its contents on the floor. The Woman does not look up as he retrieves files, memos, documents, etc. He gathers his belongings and sits in the single chair at the empty table, muttering to himself. The Woman sneaks a glance at him, checks him out, then returns to her book. He arranges his materials on the table top, a worried expression on his face, looking at some papers as if he's never seen them before. The Woman glances over again, he catches her eye. A moment, then he grins. A moment, then she smiles briefly, before returning to her book. He watches her for a while, then rises and crosses to her.

MAN. Excuse me.
WOMAN. Yes.
MAN. I was wondering if I might ...
WOMAN. No.
MAN. But —
WOMAN. I said no and I meant no. Do you have a problem with that? *(Pause.)*
MAN. There's no reason to be hostile.
WOMAN. I would prefer to be left alone.
MAN. Fine. I just want to take one of these extra chairs.
WOMAN. *(Embarrassed.)* Oh.
MAN. Would you mind?

WOMAN. Of course not. I'm sorry.

MAN. I don't have any extra chairs at my table. That table over there. Directly across from us. That one.

WOMAN. Yes.

MAN. That's my table.

WOMAN. It's very nice.

MAN. Thank you. *(Pause.)* Your table is lovely.

WOMAN. Please go away now.

MAN. Of course. *(Taking chair.)* Thanks for the chair! *(He returns to his table, places his briefcase on the newly acquired chair, shuffles around in it and pulls out a portable phone. He dials a number.)* Answer, goddamnit. *(Pause.)* Ginger, honey, listen, get Skip for me, okay? Tell him to fuck the meeting, I got something he'll get a big kick out of. No, really, tell him it's me, he won't mind. Who told you never to interrupt a meeting? Macintosh? *(Laughs.)* Ginger. I am V level management, Macintosh is only R. Since when? Shit. Shit! I'm a dead man. Thanks for letting this happen, Ginger. You ever hear the word loyalty? Spare me. You're dead meat, bitch. So, we still on for tonight? Mm-hm. Will you do me a favor? Will you wear that little red number? Oh, yes. Stop it, baby, you're making me crazy. Oh. Ginger. Ouch. *(Notices that the Woman is listening.)* Hey, I can't talk right now, okay? I've got — company. Nothing to worry about. She's just this — nobody, this bimbo, I can't get rid of her. I'll call you back, I promise. Well, if not tonight, some time this year. I promise. Yeah, yeah, yeah. Babe, I gotta go. *(He puts the phone away and glances at the Woman, who looks away. After a moment, he rises and crosses to her.)* Excuse me —

WOMAN. *(Angry.)* I'm curious. Upon what exactly do you base your inordinately high opinion of yourself? Is it your complete lack of personal integrity, your history of vacuous sexual conquests, or a combination of the two?

MAN. There's also my Porsche.

WOMAN. All of which is nothing but a pitifully transparent cover for your massive feelings of inadequacy and fear of intimacy! *(She returns to her book. Pause.)*

MAN. Please, go on.

WOMAN. Just leave me alone.

MAN. But I don't want you to feel like I don't value your input.

WOMAN. Don't patronize me.

MAN. Because I made that mistake once before. *(Ruefully.)* Of course now, I can see just how she was trying to reach out to me, but then, I couldn't hear — *(A flash of anger.)* No! I *wouldn't* hear! I shut her out! I left her no alternative, she had to leave me to save herself! *(Bursting into tears.)* The best thing that ever happened to me, and I drove her away! And you know why? *Because* she was the best thing that ever happened to me! *(Hysterical.)* What does that say about me? What kind of monster am I? *(He is overcome by anguished sobs and staggers away.)*

WOMAN. Uh ...

MAN. So what if my father was cold and remote and terrified of his own emotional nature and that was the only role model I had? That's no excuse!

WOMAN. Well, no, it *is*, to some extent ...

MAN. No. Everything you said about me was true. I'm a despicable little man, and I deserve nothing more than to burn in hell for all eternity.

WOMAN. Let's not overreact. Everybody hurts people without meaning to. I'm sure you didn't do it on purpose. And your being so willing to face up to it? That takes real courage. *(She places her hand on his shoulder.)* You're not so bad, really, you're not. *(Pause.)*

MAN. You're very kind. I'm sorry to unload all this on you. I guess I really needed to talk about it.

WOMAN. It's okay.

MAN. There aren't too many people I can talk to, I mean really talk. But ... I don't know. I feel like I can talk to you about anything, for some reason. It's almost as if ... *(Embarrassed.)* never mind.

WOMAN. What?

MAN. It's almost as if I've known you my entire life.

WOMAN. Oh.

MAN. You must think I'm really stupid.

WOMAN. No, I'm — flattered.

MAN. Really?

WOMAN. Really. *(Pause.)*

MAN. Are — you expecting someone?

WOMAN. Uhm ... no.

MAN. Well, then, would you mind if —

WOMAN. You join me? Well, no. That would be fine.

MAN. No, I just wanted to know if I could take that extra chair. *(Pause.)*

WOMAN. *(Icily.)* Expecting a group?

MAN. Not really. I just like to keep my options open.

WOMAN. Fine. Go ahead.

MAN. You sure?

WOMAN. Take it.

MAN. Thanks. *(He takes the chair to his table. She sits back down, fuming. He spends a moment arranging the chairs, then another moment sitting in each one. When he finds an arrangement that is suitable, he pulls a copy of* Playboy *out of his briefcase and starts perusing it. The Woman, having watched all this, rises and crosses to him.)*

WOMAN. Excuse me.

MAN. Oh, hi. I don't believe we've been formally introduced —

WOMAN. I need to express some of the anger, frustration, humiliation and resentment you have made me feel, in the short time that we haven't even known each other —

MAN. Hold it. You mean the anger, frustration, humiliation and resentment that you *perceive* me to have made you feel, don't you?

WOMAN. Yes.

MAN. Your feelings are your own responsibility, you know.

WOMAN. I accept that.

MAN. Good for you!

WOMAN. And if I don't express them, they will remain bottled up until they erupt in some completely inappropriate action which, if I were a man, would probably result in violence towards others weaker than myself, but since I am a woman, will more than likely be self-destructive. Frankly, I would prefer to avoid such an unpleasant scenario, having spent a large portion of my adult life — not to mention my adult income — attempting to overcome various self-destructive tendencies that were programmed into my nature by an extremely neurotic mother that I live in the hellish fear of becoming. So I am choosing, for my own sake, to express these feelings to you.

MAN. *(Considers.)* I can deal with that.

WOMAN. Good. Now. You *are* a despicable little man and you *do* deserve to rot in hell. What's more, that haircut is unfortunate, it really accentuates the cheapness of your suit, and I know you think that tie says I'm-so-hip-underneath-this-corporate-exterior , but what it really says is, I-have-the-taste-of-a-canteloupe-and-what's-more-I-need-therapy. In short, your presentation skills are laughably amateurish.

MAN. *(Impressed.)* Whoa. You play hardball. *(Suddenly there is music, kind of a '60s samba, and both the Man and Woman find themselves doing a little snake dance, much to their surprise.)*

WOMAN. Why are we doing this?

MAN. Instinct, would be my guess.

WOMAN. What instinct?

MAN. The mating instinct.

WOMAN. Oh, I'm afraid not.

MAN. Hey, I'm just as surprised as you are. But you know what they say. Rules of attraction.

WOMAN. I am in no way attracted to you.

MAN. Maybe not intellectually, although I would suspect that has something to do with it. But I could be wrong. Maybe it's purely physical.

WOMAN. You flatter yourself.

MAN. I mean, that's what it is for me. My attraction to you. Purely physical.

WOMAN. *(Flattered.)* Really?

MAN. Which is weird, because you're not my type at all.

WOMAN. And what, pray tell, is your type?

MAN. I like a tall, large-breasted, cat-eyed temptress who wears her sex like cheap perfume. And yourself?

WOMAN. I like a man who is smart, funny, confident, sensitive, affectionate, gentle, strong, independent, committed, caring, stable and willing to take risks.

MAN. Oh, *that's* realistic.

WOMAN. So I'm selective.

MAN. At least my type exists.

WOMAN. In profusion. I'll take my chances.

MAN. Statistically, you have a higher chance of —

WOMAN. Being shot by a terrorist. I know.

MAN. And you're determined to maintain this fantasy that will only create misery for you and any man you become involved with?

WOMAN. Hey, I've modified my standards considerably. I no longer require the linebacker shoulders. Lucky for you, I might add.

MAN. Oh, low blow.

WOMAN. Well, if you can have a thing for large breasts, I can have a thing for shoulders like cliffs. *(Their dancing becomes more intense.)*

MAN. I can always work out.

WOMAN. I can always get implants.

MAN. You'd do that for me?

WOMAN. Pay to be mutilated to fulfill your infantile fantasies? Why, it's every woman's dream. *(An attractive young man with linebacker shoulders enters in a waiter's uniform and joins their dance.)*

WAITER. Good afternoon. I'm your androgynous waiter.

WOMAN. *(Immediately attracted to him.)* Funny, you don't look androgynous.

WAITER. That's because I'm a woman.

WOMAN. Oh.

WAITER. My name is Dorothy. Would you care to hear about our specials today?

MAN. Just bring me the most expensive thing on the menu.

WOMAN. *I* would like to hear about the specials, Dorothy, if you don't mind. Some of us only make sixty-seven cents for every misused, undeserved dollar that others make, and therefore find it hard to justify dropping hundreds of dollars for lunch.

MAN. I'm not paying for it.

WAITER. *(Flirting.)* Well sir, I know this must seem terribly old-fashioned, but we do have a policy here of charging our customers for their meals.

MAN. Yeah? Well, I've got an unlimited expense account, toots.

WOMAN. Toots?

WAITER. *(To Man.)* You know, you're really quite attractive when you're condescending. *(The Man and the Waiter are now dancing together, completely ignoring the Woman.)*

WOMAN. No fair! I don't know how to compete with this!

MAN. Oh? I thought you weren't attracted to me.

WOMAN. I'm not! It's Dorothy that I'm after! *(Pause.)*

WAITER. *(Horrified.)* That's disgusting.

WOMAN. But —

WAITER. How dare you make such an assumption about me!

WOMAN. No, I didn't mean —

WAITER. I am not a homosexual! I am a normal, red-blooded young woman with traditional values and faith in God and country! And just because I'm slightly androgynous, you immediately jump to the conclusion that I'm a lesbian and make a pass at me? You are way out of line, sister.

WOMAN. You don't understand —

WAITER. Oh, I understand. First you confuse me with propaganda about how centuries of male oppression is really a smokescreen for men's monumental fear of women and then you promise me intimacy that men are incapable of, drawing me into your loathsome, unnatural world —

MAN. It's not *so* bad. *(Holding up his magazine.)* Got a spread in here about two stewardesses that's inspired.

WAITER. — until I surrender to unspeakable, base desires —

MAN. Can I watch?

WAITER. I am not interested in wallowing in filth and degradation! I am only interested in using sex to snag a rich husband! *(Pause.)*

WOMAN. Well, then I'm a man!

WAITER. Really?

WOMAN. Yes!
WAITER. Wow. I would never have guessed. Are you rich?
WOMAN. Filthy!
WAITER. What kind of car do you drive?
WOMAN. Well, a Porsche, naturally.
WAITER. You're married.
WOMAN. No, I'm a conspicuous bachelor!
WAITER. You're gay.
WOMAN. Oh, no! I'm notoriously heterosexual!
WAITER. Then you're one of those Peter Pan types, right? Too neurotic and ambivalent to ever make a commitment?
WOMAN. No, I dream of finding the right person to shower with financial luxury, undying devotion, and terrific sex!
WAITER. Oh! Could this be it? Could this be —
WOMAN. True love?
WAITER. Dare we even say it?
WOMAN. Overpowering us —
WAITER. Intoxicating us with its heady perfume —
WOMAN. Turning us into trembling —
WAITER. Panting —
WOMAN. Weak-kneed —
WAITER. Raw-nerved —
WOMAN. Pigs of desire!!! *(She grabs him and kisses him magnificently, forcing him to his knees. The Man has picked up the book the Woman was reading earlier and begins to read aloud from it.)*
MAN. His touch was like fire, every inch of her skin was in flames. His hungry kisses frightened her, partly from their sheer force, and partly because of the uncontrollable desire they awakened deep within her. She moaned softly — *(The Waiter moans softly.)* — and turned from him, wishing she could hide, but he took her face in his hands and said — *(The Woman mouths these words as the Man says them:.)* "No one will ever love you as I do."
WOMAN. God, I love that part.
MAN. Then, without warning, his masterful hands found their way to her delicate bosom and he ripped open the bodice of her dress, savagely ... *(The Woman tears the Waiter's shirt.*

The Man slams the book shut.) I cannot allow this to continue.
WOMAN. I was not aware your permission was required.
MAN. You were making a fool of yourself, I had to do something.
WAITER. I'm so ashamed.
WOMAN. Why?
WAITER. I feel so tawdry, so cheap ...
MAN. Slut.
WAITER. *(To Woman.)* I guess it's my own fault, I shouldn't have believed you when you said you loved me —
WOMAN. I never said I loved you. *(Lights bump up very bright, accompanied by a brash, detective-movie music sting.)*
MAN and WAITER. *(In unison, accusingly.)* What was that?
WOMAN. I didn't, all I said was, "true love — "
MAN. *(As attorney.)* Precisely my point, your honor.
WOMAN. I was merely referring to a philosophical ideal!
MAN. Your honor, the defendant plied my client with false promises and then robbed this innocent young woman of her only possession of any true worth — her virtue.
WAITER. *(In tears.)* My life is shattered.
WOMAN. Now wait just a minute. I never promised —
WAITER. You said you wanted to get married!
WOMAN. I do. Someday.
WAITER. You said you drove a Porsche.
WOMAN. I did. Once.
MAN. Your honor, I rest my case.
WOMAN. Hold it. I never actually said I loved you, or that I wanted to marry you. Now, you may have misinterpreted my statements in such a way that you heard what you wanted to hear, but I cannot be held accountable for that.
WAITER. How can you be so cruel?
WOMAN. I'm just being honest. Look. We had a good time, didn't we? Why can't that be enough? *(Screeching science fiction music. Horrified.)* Did I really just say that? *(Lights return to normal.)*
MAN. *(Triumphantly.)* Well, walk a mile in my shoes, baby. How does it feel?
WOMAN. *(Dazed.)* Not good. I think I need to sit down.

(The Man seats the Woman at his table, then takes a seat.)
WAITER. *(Gathering his tray, etc.)* Look, I'd love to stay and chat, but I have other tables to attend to.
MAN. Aren't you going to tell us the specials? *(Pause.)*
WAITER. Why don't you let me get you another waiter?
MAN. Why?
WAITER. I just think it would be best for everyone concerned. I mean, after everything we've been through —
MAN. Don't be ridiculous. We're all adults here.
WAITER. Well, I'm sure you two upwardly mobile types have shrinks you pay obscene amounts of money to help you accept and transcend humiliating episodes in your life, but me, every cent I make goes into hair care products, so I feel at somewhat of a disadvantage —
MAN. I think you're making this much more important than it is. You really didn't mean anything to either one of us. *(To Woman.)* Isn't that right?
WOMAN. *(To Waiter.)* Well ... I do have to admit to a keen aesthetic appreciation of, you know, your outward appearance, but aside from that, no. Sorry. *(Pause.)*
WAITER. That's why I would prefer you had another waiter, because this is really damaging to my self-esteem ...
MAN. *(Good-naturedly.)* Oh, grow up. Don't you think you're taking this a little seriously? Look at yourself. You're just another well-put-together bimbo. People use you, that's the function you serve in society, okay? It's not so bad. Play your cards right, you can probably get your own television show.
WOMAN. There's really no need to be so brutal.
MAN. Why not? Why not? That's the problem with this culture, everybody expects too much. Not everybody can be happy. Can you imagine what that would be like? People would no longer feel compelled to acquire material goods in a futile attempt to fill the void in their lives! Advertising would become completely ineffectual! The economy would collapse!
WOMAN. The economy *is* collapsing.
MAN. Oh, right. Turn this into an emotional thing. That is just like a woman.

WAITER. I still think it would be best if another waiter —

MAN. Look, do you want me to talk to your manager? Stop whining and just tell us the specials. *(Pause.)*

WAITER. Well, we have two specials today. We have the new commitment —

WOMAN. Oh, that sounds interesting.

MAN. I'm allergic to it.

WAITER. And we have mindless promiscuity with a drug and alcohol glaze.

MAN. There we go. How much is that?

WAITER. It's the most expensive thing on the menu.

MAN. Then it's got my name on it.

WAITER. *(Pulling a legal form out of his vest pocket.)* Very well. I'll just need your signature on this release form. *(Pause. The Man looks at the release form for a long time.)*

MAN. I think I may want to change my order. *(To Woman.)* You go ahead.

WOMAN. I'll have the new commitment, please. How is that prepared?

WAITER. No one really knows. And for you, sir?

MAN. I'm going to need some more time. Can you come back in just a few minutes?

WAITER. Oh, certainly. Allow me to readjust my entire routine to suit you.

MAN. Thank you.

WAITER. Because of my vastly inferior socioeconomic status.

MAN. Yes.

WAITER. I exist only to serve.

MAN. And that's as it should be.

WAITER. It is my privilege. *(He exits.)*

MAN. That girl has a hell of a future ahead of her. *(Pause. The Woman glares at him.)* Oh, don't look at me like that. After the way you treated her?

WOMAN. I cannot be held accountable for my actions. I was a man at the time.

MAN. *(Conspiratorially.)* So, how'd you like it?

WOMAN. It was interesting.

MAN. Interesting? Didn't you have any fun?

WOMAN. I guess it was exciting.

MAN. Yeah! Isn't it a rush? Stretching the limits, seeing how much you can get away with?

WOMAN. Definitely educational.

MAN. Educational? Are you kidding me?

WOMAN. In kind of a depraved way. It's not for me, though.

MAN. Yeah, well I can see that.

WOMAN. No. Too tense, too competitive, too many insecurities.

MAN. Couldn't hack it, huh?

WOMAN. Feeling that defensive all the time? Who would want to?

MAN. Well, it takes a man to be a man. *(Pause.)*

WOMAN. *(Exploding.)* God, I am so sick of hearing that!

MAN. What?

WOMAN. Being a man! Like it's more important than being a person!

MAN. Calm down —

WOMAN. I will not calm down! It's so senseless, all you poor little boys, getting all twisted and repressed and neurotic by trying to grow up to be men!

MAN. Well, what would you like for us to grow up to be?

WOMAN. People! Human beings! But no! Be a man about it! Walk like a man! Take it like a man! You're too strong to ever need anybody, and too cool to ever be affected by anything! You're full of resentment and rage and frustration and fear, but you're too stupid to do anything more constructive with it than kill somebody or blow something up!

MAN. I never killed anybody!

WOMAN. And then being rewarded for that kind of behavior, you've been groomed for it from day one!

MAN. I don't even own a gun!

WOMAN. What, is that supposed to impress me?

MAN. But —

WOMAN. When the hellish nightmare of Armageddon is finally realized, the blood of millions will be on your hands and your hands alone!

MAN. You can't possibly ask me to shoulder the blame for that!

WOMAN. Running away from responsibility? How typically male!

MAN. Blaming men for everything that's wrong with the world? How typically female!

WOMAN. I just call it as I see it, Buster.

MAN. Okay! Okay! If men are so rotten, then why are you trying so hard to be one?

WOMAN. Once! That was once!

MAN. Oh, come on! Look at you! What is that get-up? What is this thing, here? *(He indicates the conservative bow she wears at the collar of her blouse.)* This poof thing, this ridiculous tie substitute!

WOMAN. I'll tell you what that is. It's a superficial and totally absurd symbol that one must display to be taken seriously in the male-dominated business world. It says, I don't make waves, I toe the line, I'm a slave to the machine.

MAN. Well, for somebody who is so contemptuous of men, it seems to me that you're pretty damn eager to play the same bullshit, sell-out conformity game.

WOMAN. Oh, *I* see. It's okay for *you* to be a sniveling, brown-nosing corporate sycophant, but it's not okay for me?

MAN. Well, yes.

WOMAN. That's quite an ugly double standard.

MAN. You're nothing but a jealous, spiteful harpy!

WOMAN. And you're a swollen, self-important jackass!

MAN. Brainless twit!

WOMAN. Spineless dork!

MAN. Feeb!

WOMAN. Geek!

MAN. Twink!

WOMAN. Dink! *(Suddenly there is more '60s samba music, and they find themselves doing the same little snake dance.)* Oh, no, not again.

MAN. Can't fight nature, baby.

WOMAN. This is in no way natural.

MAN. Stop resisting your true feelings!

WOMAN. Remind me what those are.
MAN. You want me. You need me. You ache for me.
WOMAN. You're out of your mind.
MAN. So why do you continue to dance with me?
WOMAN. You'll have to forgive me, it seems to be some kind of involuntary, knee-jerk reaction to this music.
MAN. God, I love a Pavlovian woman. *(Without warning, the music changes into a Slavic folk tune. The Man and Woman adjust their dancing likewise. The music then changes to a frenzied slam dance number, then to a Strauss waltz, and then finally to the throbbing beat of African drums. The Man and Woman get carried away, dancing with wild hedonistic abandon. Suddenly the music stops. The Woman staggers to her chair. The Man realizes he is dancing alone and stops.)* Hey, what gives?
WOMAN. *(Refusing to look at him.)* The music stopped.
MAN. So?
WOMAN. I just don't see much point in dancing without music. Is that such a crime?
MAN. *(Crossing to her.)* We can always make our own music —
WOMAN. *(Suddenly, inappropriately hysterical.)* Listen to me! I am in no way attracted to you! The mere thought of anything romantic or sexual between the two of us makes me nauseous! I wouldn't consider it if you were the last man on earth, and I had spent two years alone on a desert island eating nothing but raw oysters and listening to Prince music! I'd rather be torn to pieces by wild dogs! It's just not in the realm of possibility, do you understand me? Never in a million years, no way, not on your life, no chance in hell, get it out of your head! Am I making myself clear? *(Pause. The Man seems impressed.)*
MAN. Would you be willing to put that in writing?
WOMAN. Gladly. *(He pulls a legal form out of his briefcase.)*
MAN. Okay, just sign here — here — here — here — here — here — and here. *(She does so.)* Well, now that we've taken care of *that* — *(He drops to his knees. Fervently.)* I love you intensely, completely, and without reservation.
WOMAN. What?
MAN. The moment I saw you my life changed forever. I was

only sleepwalking before, just a shadow of myself. But you have touched something in me I forgot even existed —

WOMAN. You're hallucinating.

MAN. I burn for you, my heart aches for you, I close my eyes and see you, only you, I worship you, I cherish you, God! How I adore you! You must love me or I shall die.

WOMAN. *(Horrified.)* Stop that!

MAN. I can't help myself!

WOMAN. Well, try!

MAN. I would give up the world for you, but you're asking me to do the one thing I'm incapable of!

WOMAN. I know! Behaving like a rational being!

MAN. *(Jumps onto a chair.)* I cannot silence my love for you!

WOMAN. You are doing the worst thing a man can do to a woman. You are saying all the right things! And I won't stand for it! Do you hear me?

MAN. I want the entire world to know! *(Rock and roll music is heard amidst the screams of hordes of adolescent girls, and a spotlight focuses on the Man as he begins to lip-sync to a rock 'n' roll love song. The Woman watches, amazed, for a moment, then angrily pushes him off the chair. The music ends abruptly, as if someone pulled the needle of a record. Pause.)* What the hell did you do that for?

WOMAN. Because if you think I'm impressed by some adolescent fantasy that, one, you're too old for and two, has absolutely nothing to do with me, you are playing this game with some seriously depleted resources.

MAN. *(Shaken.)* You can't possibly mean that!

WOMAN. You bet I do, Bonzo. I've seen this movie too many times.

MAN. But you — you are my life —

WOMAN. Thanks, but mine is already weird enough.

MAN. *(Desperate.)* What can I do to make you stay?

WOMAN. Not a damn thing, pal, that's the point. Get it? *(She turns to leave.)*

MAN. No one will ever love you as much as I do. *(This stops her.)*

WOMAN. Oh yeah? *(She turns to him, then leans against the*

table provocatively.) So take me. *(Pause.)*

MAN. Excuse me?

WOMAN. Take me right here. On the table. *(The Man laughs nervously.)* I want you. I need you. I ache for you.

MAN. But —

WOMAN. I'm hungry for you, baby.

MAN. Well, lunch is coming, we don't want to spoil our appetites, do we? *(The Woman runs her hands over her body.)*

WOMAN. *(A sex kitten squeal.)* Oh, hurry, please don't keep me waiting —

MAN. What the hell's gotten into you?

WOMAN. Nothing, yet, but I'm working on it. *(She laughs and starts toward him slowly.)*

MAN. Hey, stay right there.

WOMAN. Come on, you know you want to.

MAN. No, I don't, really —

WOMAN. It's too late to turn back, you got me all worked up.

MAN. It was an accident, I never meant — *(She grabs him by the tie and pulls him to her.)*

WOMAN. Get ready, stud boy. It's about time somebody taught you how to ride. *(Terrified, the Man reaches into his briefcase and pulls out the form the Woman previously signed.)*

MAN. What about this? *(The Woman takes it, looks at it, then rips it apart.)* Hey! I made that agreement with you in good faith!

WOMAN. So sue me. *(She undoes his tie and pulls it off; he grabs her hand. A standoff. They stare at each other intently, then their lips meet violently, as if pulled together by magnetic force. They kiss for a long time, practically mauling each other with abandon at first, then gradually giving way to affection and tenderness until finally their lips slowly part. A moment as they look at each other with wonder, smiling shyly, then suddenly the Man steps back, an expression of uncontrollable fear on his face.)*

MAN. Whoa. I need some space. *(He crosses to his table and sits. The Woman stands stunned, then crosses to him.)*

WOMAN. Excuse me, what just happened?

MAN. In God's name, stop suffocating me!

WOMAN. What?

MAN. You want too much from me!

WOMAN. How do you know what I want?

MAN. *(With painful sincerity.)* Look. I'm just not ready for a relationship right now. I could pretend like I was, but that wouldn't be fair to either one of us, would it? I'm sorry. *(A voluptuous young woman enters wearing a uniform identical to the one worn by the Waiter, with her shirt ripped in the same place. She places a platter on the Woman's table.)* Excuse me. *(He crosses to Waitress.)* Hi. Want to get married?

WAITRESS. I can't, I'm working.

WOMAN. I don't believe this.

MAN. *(To Woman.)* Oh, listen, we can still be friends, right?

WOMAN. You are such a gutless chickenshit son of a bitch.

MAN. *(To Woman.)* You know, you have excellent communication skills. So go communicate somewhere, okay?

WOMAN. Oh, right. That would be really convenient, wouldn't it.

MAN. Uh, yes, actually.

WOMAN. You're probably used to women making things convenient for you.

MAN. As a matter of fact —

WOMAN. Starting with your mother, I bet. *(The Waitress sighs loudly and turns to leave.)*

MAN. Excuse me. *(Grabs Waitress.)* Please. Don't go away. *(Back to Woman, impatient.)* Are we finished?

WOMAN. Look. I am not here to make things easy for you. But I *am* here, and I was here before *you* were. And I am not ready to leave.

MAN. Fine. Suit yourself.

WOMAN. Believe it or not, there's a part of me that wants to watch.

MAN. Doesn't bother me.

WOMAN. It's that same part of me that can't help staring at car wrecks.

MAN. I hope you're speaking for someone else's benefit, because I'm not listening. *(To Waitress.)* Hi.

WAITRESS. Hello.

MAN. Will you join me for a drink?

WAITRESS. No. I could lose my job.

MAN. Whatever you're making, I'll double it.

WAITRESS. Oh. Okay. *(They sit.)*

MAN. What would you like?

WAITRESS. Oh, I don't drink.

MAN. What about lunch?

WAITRESS. I'm on a diet.

MAN. Isn't there anything you want?

WAITRESS. My own TV show.

MAN. It's yours.

WAITRESS. You mean it?

MAN. Piece of cake.

WAITRESS. Thanks.

MAN. So what's your name?

WAITRESS. You don't remember me?

MAN. *(Lying.)* Of course I remember you! How could I forget you? How long has it been?

WAITRESS. Oh, about ten minutes. *(Pause.)*

MAN. Wait a minute —

WAITRESS. That's right. I'm your waiter, Dorothy. Well, I go by Donald now.

MAN. I don't think I —

WAITRESS. I had a sex change operation, and now I'm a man. *(The Woman laughs; the Man glances at her, irritated. Pause.)*

MAN. *(To Waitress.)* Are you sure about that?

WAITRESS. Oh, yes. I know, maybe it was a little drastic, but I was so tired of constantly being mistaken for a man, and being depressed about it all the time. So I decided well, maybe there's something to it, I must radiate some kind of male energy, and then somebody told me that if you have a sex change operation they would make a TV movie about your life and you would get to play yourself in it, so I did it. It's more of a career move than anything else.

MAN. Well, it certainly suits you.

WAITRESS. Thank you.

MAN. As a matter of fact, magnificent is the word that comes to mind.

WAITRESS. Oh, go on.
MAN. Or perhaps god-like.
WAITRESS. I bet you say that to all the boys.
MAN. Actually, I'm quite hard to impress. *(Modestly.)* I'm kind of a connoisseur of beautiful men.
WAITRESS. Really?
MAN. Yes. Some women paint, some women shop. I ... appreciate beauty. *(Pause.)*
WAITRESS. You're a woman.
MAN. Oh, yes.
WAITRESS. I'm sorry, I thought you were a man. *(The Man looks away, seemingly embarrassed.)*
MAN. A lot of people make that mistake.
WAITRESS. Oh, you poor thing, I know —
MAN. I thought you of all people would understand.
WAITRESS. *(Taking his hand.)* Believe me, I do.
MAN. I know you do. *(Turning to her.)* I feel as if I've known you my entire life.
WOMAN. I'm going to be sick.
MAN. *(To Woman.)* Oh, can't you bear to let somebody else be happy, just once?
WOMAN. No, listen, really. I'm happy that you're happy. Really.
MAN. You mean that?
WOMAN. Yes.
MAN. *(Touched.)* Thank you. That means a lot to me.
WOMAN. It doesn't mean jack shit, asshole, I just want you out of my life.
MAN. *(Hurt.)* Fine, you got a deal.
WOMAN. Good.
MAN. Terrific.
WOMAN. Better. *(Returns to her table, finds platter.)* What's this?
WAITRESS. That's the new commitment. *(The Woman flings the platter from the stage.)*
MAN. *(To Waitress.)* Now, where were we?
WAITRESS. Can I be honest with you?
MAN. *(Uncomfortable.)* If you feel like you have to.

WAITRESS. As we were talking just now, I found myself fantasizing about you as a Roman gladiator and me as a naive but devastatingly beautiful young slave boy.

MAN. That's really creative.

WAITRESS. Of course, I realize it's out of the question.

MAN. Oh, no, it isn't.

WAITRESS. Are you kidding? Barf, gack, puke my guts out. *(The Man appears crestfallen.)* Please don't get me wrong. I think you're a lovely person, and very attractive. It's just that I'm not into women.

MAN. Oh! Well, no problem, because I'm — I really am a man.

WAITRESS. But you just said that you were a woman.

MAN. I was —

WOMAN. He was lying through his teeth, sister, that's what he was doing!

WAITRESS. *(Turning on her.)* Oh, you're one to talk.

WOMAN. Me?

WAITRESS. Don't think I've forgotten the abysmal treatment I received at your hands! Thanks to you, I'm scarred for life! Well, partly thanks to you, and partly thanks to a marvelous plastic surgeon. *(To Man.)* I hope you weren't lying to me, because that's one thing I cannot forgive. *(She glares at the Woman.)*

MAN. I wasn't, I — I am a woman, but — I'm trapped in a man's body!

WAITRESS. *(Excited.)* God, we have so much in common.

MAN. So you know what I'm going through —

WAITRESS. Yes!

MAN. — being held hostage by a cruel twist of fate —

WAITRESS. Well, actually, it wasn't fate for me, it was a conscious decision, and I don't regret it, either.

MAN. So, want to come over to my place and watch some Gladiator movies?

WAITRESS. Oh, I don't see you as a gladiator anymore.

MAN. You don't?

WAITRESS. No, I see you as a sadistic jail warden in a small Southern town.

MAN. That's the nicest thing anyone has ever said to me.

WAITRESS. I'm a naive but devastatingly beautiful young farm boy falsely accused of a crime I did not commit, being held without bail, in solitary confinement.

MAN. Caged heat?

WAITRESS. Precisely. It's 98 degrees and there's no air conditioning.

MAN. Your clothes are soaked through and hug your ripe young body like second skin —

WAITRESS. I can't see your eyes behind your mirrored aviator sunglasses, but I feel them all over me like a rash —

WOMAN. That's revolting.

MAN. You ask me for a drink of water —

WAITRESS. You pull your keys out of your tight jail-warden pants and unlock the door —

MAN. It swings open slowly —

WAITRESS. My heart is pounding —

MAN. You lower your eyes as I enter your cell —

WAITRESS. You hand me the water but you don't let go —

MAN. You look up at me, frightened —

WAITRESS. You take my hand and place it on your belt —

MAN. You smile, and I think maybe you're not as naive as you let on —

WAITRESS. And you're right, because then I pull your gun out of its holster and I shoot you in the face.

MAN. You what?!

WAITRESS. Your body crumples to the cold cement floor, jerking hideously in a death spasm —

MAN. Wait a minute —

WAITRESS. I walk out of the jail, cool as a cucumber, steal your car and drive to the Trailways station, where Tom Brokaw is waiting for me. He takes me in his arms and his boyish yet distinguished face lights up as he says, "I have left my wife, my children, my prestigious and lucrative career for you. Please run away with me to the coast of Italy where we shall live in an olive grove, drink wine and make love all day." And I say, "That's sweet, Tom, but that's just not what I had in mind." He's crushed and he hurls himself under an oncoming bus. I feel really bad, and collapse into one of those chairs with the TV built into it, and then I hear someone say, "Please don't cry, you're breaking my heart," and I look up, and it's Mel Gibson, wearing nothing but Saran Wrap. "I won't leave my wife," he says. "I won't leave my children, or my lucrative career, but I will spend obscene amounts of money on you and see you when I can, at least until we get bored with each other." And I say, "When that happens, do I still get to keep everything you've given me?" And he says, "Yes." And I look long and hard into his blue eyes, eyes bluer than the sky, so blue it looks like nature messed up somehow, and I can see he's telling the truth. And I say, "That's more like it." *(Pause.)*

WOMAN. Well, you've certainly become craven and opportunistic.

WAITRESS. Damn straight. I'm tired of being everybody's doormat. I'm out for everything I can get.

MAN. I think your change in attitude is admirable.

WOMAN. I think it's sad.

MAN. You would.

WAITRESS. What a wimp.

WOMAN. You two deserve each other.

MAN. *(To Waitress.)* What do you say we go back to my office and engage in some mutually craven and opportunistic sex?

WAITRESS. I'm game. Maybe later, we can talk about that television show.

MAN. *(Uncomfortably.)* Oh, yeah. Right.

WOMAN. Here, take this. *(She hands him his tie.)*

MAN. But I gave this to you, I want you to keep it.

WOMAN. You need it more than I do.

MAN. But —

WOMAN. Take it. *(He shrugs and joins the Waitress.)*

MAN. *(To Waitress.)* I'll never understand women.

WAITRESS. That was a woman?

MAN. Yeah.

WAITRESS. I'm really confused now. *(They exit.)*

WOMAN. Asshole. *(She picks up her book and reads for a few moments then puts it down. Pause. She opens her briefcase and pulls out a cassette recorder, sets it on the table and turns it on.)*

TAPE. Hello! Welcome to Motivational Magic. Let's start with ten simple Steps to Success. Number one. Objectively assess your level of power within your organization. Identify those who are more powerful than you are — we'll call these "the in crowd," people that you would like to impress, be accepted by and eventually obliterate on your way to the top. Next, identify those who are less powerful than you. We'll call these individuals "scum of the earth," pathetic weaklings you can terrorize and humiliate, while increasing your self-confidence and sharpening your leadership skills. Number two. If you have any personal friends among the scum of the earth, dump them immediately. I cannot stress the importance of this. If possible, get them fired. That way, you won't be reminded of your former friendship, which could lead to sentimental feelings of guilt and remorse, something to be avoided at all costs. Number three. Volunteer assistance to the in crowd whenever the opportunity presents itself. Flatter them shamelessly. Sleep with them if you can, and try to elicit incriminating personal information when they are most vulnerable. You may want to blackmail them later, or even have them arrested — *(The Woman, who has been listening with growing horror, turns off the tape player abruptly. Almost instinctively, her hand grabs the conservative bow at the neck of her blouse. She flings it to the floor and stomps on it in a frenzy, crying out and making savage guttural noises. Gradually she stops and stands there in a daze. After a moment, the Man enters, despondent. He glances at her, then crosses to her table.)*

MAN. *(Indicating the one remaining chair at her table.)* Excuse me, can I take this chair? *(She turns to him, too dazed to be angry.)*

WOMAN. It's the only one I have left.

MAN. Can I take it?

WOMAN. Why do you want it?

MAN. Because I don't have it. *(She sighs.)*

WOMAN. Fine. Go ahead.

MAN. Thanks. *(He takes it to his table and sits, despondently.*

The Woman reconsiders and crosses to his table.)

WOMAN. I changed my mind.

MAN. What?

WOMAN. You can have one of these, but I'm taking two back.

MAN. But then we'll both have the same number.

WOMAN. That's right.

MAN. No, no. This is a completely unacceptable situation.

WOMAN. It's called reality. *(She takes the chair.)*

MAN. *(Standing.)* I'm afraid I can't allow you to do that.

WOMAN. Come one step closer to me and I'll mother you. *(The Man steps back, frightened. Pause.)*

MAN. You do and I'll let you. *(The Woman steps back, frightened. Pause.)*

WOMAN. You're bluffing.

MAN. Only one way to find out. *(A tense pause, then the Woman approaches the Man as if to embrace him.)*

WOMAN. Come here, you poor baby. Let Mommy smother you. *(The Man grimaces, then throws himself into her arms.)*

MAN. Gosh, Mom, this is great. I don't ever want to grow up. *(The Woman screams; the Man screams; they break apart and run to opposite sides of the stage.)*

WOMAN. Don't ever do that to me again!

MAN. You started it!

WOMAN. I did not. You're the chair pig! You're the one who won't stop until he has everything and nobody else has anything!

MAN. I can't help that! That's part of my biological nature!

WOMAN. Bullshit! You are entirely capable of being emotionally open, kind and generous!

MAN. Oh, sure. Everybody else is out grabbing everything they can get their hands on, fucking over everybody else in the process, and I'm supposed to just give something away?

WOMAN. Yes.

MAN. *(Mystified.)* Why should I?

WOMAN. Because you can. *(Pause. The Man suddenly kicks a chair angrily.)*

MAN. *(Exploding.)* God! I hate that Hallmark card, little-engine-that-could, may-the-road-rise-up-and-slap-you-in-the-fucking-face bullshit!

WOMAN. That's right. Get a little too close to the truth, something you don't want to look at, and what happens? You turn into a cornered animal, lashing out at whatever you can, just as long as it's not bigger than you and it can't fight back.

MAN. So what do you want me to be? Mr. Sensitive? Fine. I'll be happy to share my feelings with you. I'd love to show you just how fucking freaked out I really am, how my life is barely held together and at any minute the whole thing might just snap, and you can watch me when I just fall apart, and I will, because deep down, as deep as it gets, I know I don't have what it takes. I'm not talking about what it takes to be the best at everything, or what it takes to make an indelible mark on the world. Fuck that. I don't have what it takes to go across the street and buy a cup of coffee. Everybody else does, but not me. Because I'm missing — something. I don't know what it is, but I do know one thing. I know that sometimes I understand how a man could pick up a shotgun and go into a Burger King and just start spraying bullets. I would never do that. At least I don't think I would. But I can relate, you hear what I'm saying? *(Pause.)* Is this better?

WOMAN. Uh —

MAN. Not exactly what you had in mind, is it?

WOMAN. Well —

MAN. I didn't think so. *(Picks up romance novel, reading from it.)* "His smile was the smile of a man whose heart, though scarred, remained open and always would remain open to the wonders of life and the miracle of love. And as he stood there, the last rays of the setting sun casting a golden glow across his brow, she knew that she had come home at last, that she would always be safe with this well-spring of strength, this marvelous protector, this man she loved." *(He drops the book onto the table and looks at Woman bitterly. She looks back at him, then gets up, gathers her things silently, and turns to leave.)* Wait —

WOMAN. What? You don't need me here. You've already decided that my expectations are so unrealistic no man could possibly live up to them, you've made up your mind that I would reject you, all that's left is for you to feel sorry for yourself. You don't need me for that. *(Picks up book.)* You think this is what I want? Get myself a good man, all my problems will just disappear? That is so fucking arrogant I could puke. I have a life, thank you. *(Turns to leave.)* Oh, I'll admit, I do want somebody. Somebody who is smart, somebody who is real, somebody who doesn't turn into the Human Clam the minute things start to get too close. Because I am just as freaked out as you are, but just once, just *once* I want to feel like maybe I'm not totally alone in the world, that there's somebody next to me who's every bit as scared as I am but who will do what he can to keep me from losing sight of what's good, and let me do the same for him. That's all. But that would require someone like you looking at someone like me and accepting me for who I am, wouldn't it? And of course, statistically speaking, we both know there's a higher chance of me discovering nuclear fusion in a curling iron after being the first woman to win both the Miss America Pageant and the Presidential Election.

MAN. Well —

WOMAN. Do you mind if I look at your magazine?

MAN. I —

WOMAN. Thank you. *(Opens to centerfold.)* My, my. Isn't she a testament to the art of airbrushing. Oh, look, she has her own data sheet. Isn't that sweet? May I? *(Reads.)* "Name: Brandy McKenna. Age: Twenty-three. Ambitions: To get as much out of life as I can while helping others get what they want and to be in a Motley Crue video. Turn-ons: Saunas and massages, cute cuddly animals, sun-bathing, giving myself totally to the man I love." The girl should be a saint. Saint Brandy. "Ideal man: Knows what he wants and isn't afraid to go after it. Likes to party. Drives a Porsche." Well, I think Brandy speaks for all women. *(Pause. She puts down the magazine.)* Works both ways.

MAN. It's only a magazine.

WOMAN. *(Indicating romance novel.)* It's only a book. *(Long pause. They look at each other apprehensively, eventually smiling in spite of themselves.)*

MAN. Okay. Okay, so I don't drive a Porsche.

WOMAN. You don't?

MAN. No. I drive a *(Mumbles something unintelligible.)*

WOMAN. A what?

MAN. A *(Mumbles something unintelligible.)*

WOMAN. I still didn't hear —

MAN. I drive a Vega!

WOMAN. Oh.

MAN. Hatchback.

WOMAN. I'm really sorry. *(They laugh.)* So now what do we do?

MAN. Beats me. You got an idea?

WOMAN. I haven't got a clue.

MAN. I'm still hungry.

WOMAN. Me too.

MAN. You want to go somewhere else?

WOMAN. Yes. The service here is — a little unnerving.

MAN. You can say that again.

WOMAN. What happened to your thing with the waiter?

MAN. Oh. I got dumped.

WOMAN. I'm sorry.

MAN. Don't be. I was bored out of my mind. I only stuck around because it was easier not to do anything about it.

WOMAN. I've done that.

MAN. Why are we so fucked up?

WOMAN. Who knows? Who cares? Let's get out of here. *(They stand to leave. Suddenly there is strange, ethereal music; the Waiter and Waitress enter. They move as if in a dream and drop off the check at the Man's table.)*

WAITER. Please pay the cashier on your way out.

WAITRESS. Have a nice day! *(They dance off. Music ends.)*

MAN. *(Picks up check.)* I'll get it.

WOMAN. *(Takes it from him.)* No, no. Let me.

MAN. Please, it's the least I can do.

WOMAN. You didn't even order.

MAN. I had a drink at the bar.

WOMAN. Really. This is my treat.

MAN. I can't let you do that.

WOMAN. I have to tell you that it really bothers me when you say you can't let me do something. I don't need your permission.

MAN. That's not what I meant —

WOMAN. That's what it sounded like.

MAN. Why are you always so quick to accuse me?

WOMAN. I'm not accusing you of anything. I'm merely pointing out your behavior.

MAN. Oh, thank you so much. It's really helpful, having someone who knows me so much better than myself, as you do, constantly explain myself to me.

WOMAN. There's no need to be sarcastic.

MAN. You're right. You're absolutely right, about everything. You're a genius, I'm an asshole. Are you happy?

WOMAN. I do not assume to be a genius, but I think it's safe to say the other half of your statement is correct.

MAN. Pay the damn check. I don't give a shit.

WOMAN. Oh, no. I wouldn't dream of wounding your precious pride. By all means, you pay it.

MAN. Maybe I don't want to. Maybe I'm tired of always picking up the tab just because I'm the man.

WOMAN. Well, then, what is this whole thing about?

MAN. Give me that. *(He grabs the check but she refuses to let go; the check gets ripped in half.)*

WOMAN. Now look what you've done, you pompous bastard!

MAN. Me? You're the one who wouldn't let go, you ignorant slut!

WOMAN. Fuck you, you cheesy dickhead!

MAN. Same to you, you sniveling bitch! *(Suddenly, there is music, the same '60s samba. They look at each other in horror and scream.)*

BLACKOUT

PROPERTY LIST

Briefcase (WOMAN) with:
- paperback romance novel
- cassette recorder

Briefcase (MAN) with:
- papers
- documents
- portable phone
- *Playboy* magazine
- legal form

Tray (WAITRESS)
Legal release form (WAITER)
'New commitment' platter
Meal check (WAITER)

SOUND EFFECTS

Screams of young girls at a rock 'n roll concert

THE M WORD

THE M WORD was first produced by the Lucille Ball Festival of New Comedy (David Munnell, Artistic Director) at the Reg Lenna Civic Center in Jamestown, New York, on May 24, 1991. It was directed by Andrew Weisnet; the scene design was by Gary Eckhart; the lighting design was by David A. Holcomb; the costume design was by Mary Ann Powell; the sound design was by Elliott Forrest and the production stage manager was Keith Schmitt. The cast was as follows:

WOMAN .... Mary Kane
MAN .... Michael Cooke

CHARACTERS

WOMAN, Well-groomed, early thirties. Wears an expensive, tailored business suit. Any race.

MAN, Well-groomed, early thirties. Wears an expensive, tailored business suit. Any race.

SETTING

An tastefully decorated office in a large corporation in New York City. A desk and chair, another chair downstage of the desk. Elsewhere, a table or file cabinet on which sits a pitcher of water and two empty glasses.

THE M WORD

An office. A well-groomed Woman in a business suit sits at her desk, working furiously. Elsewhere in the office is a table or file cabinet on which sits a pitcher of water and two empty glasses. A Man in a business suit appears at the door, carrying a large, official-looking document and a personal notebook. He knocks to get her attention.

WOMAN. Yes?

MAN. Are you terribly busy?

WOMAN. Well —

MAN. This won't take long. *(She puts her work aside and motions him to come in.)*

WOMAN. I can give you ten minutes. I have a very important presentation this afternoon.

MAN. Don't worry. I'm catching the three o'clock shuttle to D.C., which means I'll need to be out of here by — *(He performs some calculations on his wristwatch.)* — one forty-eight at the absolute latest.

WOMAN. I really admire a man who allocates his time efficiently.

MAN. I'll get right to the point. We've been working together for six months, three days, fourteen hours and — *(Checks his watch again.)* — twenty-two seconds. During that time, I believe we have grown to enjoy each other's company —

WOMAN. I wouldn't necessarily say *enjoy* ...

MAN. Really.

WOMAN. It implies a level of passion we have yet to achieve.

MAN. Oh, well, of course. I didn't mean to paint this as an

emotional thing.

WOMAN. I'm glad to hear you say that.

MAN. On the contrary, one of the things I value in our relationship is the complete lack of spontaneity, which virtually eliminates any element of surprise. I know in advance how you're going to react, and I'm able to plan my strategies accordingly.

WOMAN. And I can predict your strategies without fail, thus being able to manipulate you effortlessly, without your even knowing it. There is real security in that.

MAN. We have a lot to offer each other.

WOMAN. We keep each other on our toes.

MAN. Shall I mention the M word now?

WOMAN. Oh, no. Much too soon. You'd do better to keep the suspense going for a little while longer.

MAN. I admire your coaching skills. And I am secure enough in my masculinity not to be threatened by your criticism.

WOMAN. I appreciate that. *(Pause.)*

MAN. *(Consults his notebook.)* Well, let me begin by saying I don't particularly enjoy sex with you, which I view as a positive, since there's no danger of my becoming obsessed and surrendering my psychic power.

WOMAN. Usually I pretend you're someone else when we're making love. It's the only way I can get through it.

MAN. I can live with that. As long as you don't broadcast your feelings within my peer group.

WOMAN. Agreed.

MAN. I need a woman to take to the Hamptons this summer. You're quite presentable in a bathing suit —

WOMAN. Thank you.

MAN. — and could arouse feelings of jealousy in other men with whom I compete for advancement in my social circle. One question: are you interested in producing offspring?

WOMAN. My biological clock is ticking like mad.

MAN. Have you given any thought as to what qualities you seek in a potential procreative partner?

WOMAN. Any man who is straight, has a steady job and is

not a mass murderer looks pretty damn good. Of course, these are preliminary projections. I would need to conduct a much more extensive study before actually undertaking such a challenging project.

MAN. Understood.

WOMAN. And yourself? What are your feelings on the issue?

MAN. Well, of course I want children.

WOMAN. Why?

MAN. Oh, many reasons. First, they're quite a prestige item these days.

WOMAN. Uh-huh.

MAN. Second, they would greatly reinforce my own and others' notions of my virility.

WOMAN. Uh-huh.

MAN. Third, I have many unresolved issues with my dead father that I could work out with a son of my own.

WOMAN. Uh-huh.

MAN. And fourth, I've always enjoyed pets.

WOMAN. What are your feelings on shared child-rearing duties?

MAN. Ah ... I'm open to the *concept.* I certainly plan to budget frequent parcels of quality time for the kids, but ... I guess I'm not sure what you mean exactly by shared child-rearing duties. Would you care to elaborate?

WOMAN. Will you agree to a quota system that ensures even distribution of diaper-changing responsibilities? Are you willing to begin networking *immediately* in order to improve a child's chances of getting into an Ivy League pre-school? Are you willing to undergo sensitivity training yourself in order to become a more nurturing parent and role model, thus alleviating some of the historical burden of which mothers carry a disproportionate share? *(Pause.)*

MAN. Can I think about that?

WOMAN. Of course, I don't think we have to come to any decision today.

MAN. Great. *(Checks his pad.)* As far as economic considerations go, I am confident that our combined income would be formidable, and we can continue our futile attempt to fill the void in our lives with overpriced material goods.

WOMAN. That's all well and good, but I think that if we work together on this, using a mixture of jurisprudence and selective risk-taking, we should be able to make the leap from upwardly mobile to wealthy before we're forty-five.

MAN. Oh, I plan to become a millionaire before I'm forty.

WOMAN. Really. That doesn't give you much time.

MAN. I'm aware of that.

WOMAN. May I ask what your contingency plans are?

MAN. I'm considering several options, including suicide in the event of not achieving my goal.

WOMAN. An aggressive approach.

MAN. I work best when I'm under pressure.

WOMAN. Hmm. I would be forty myself at that time, still young enough to embark on a new life partnership. Trouble is, most of the men whom I would deem appropriate partners will be just beginning their mid-life crises, and will therefore be interested only in very young women who make them feel less anxiety about their own mortality. On the other hand, I could do a Cher thing, and take as a lover a man half my age, involved in some kind of manual labor. And preferably not too bright. Hmm. I doubt if such a thing would go over well here at work, but ... if you have a good life insurance policy I *could* stop working altogether. Maybe. Hmm. I'll need to think about this some more.

MAN. Of course.

WOMAN. By the way, have you planned your own mid-life crisis yet?

MAN. Not fully, but I have settled on a basic approach.

WOMAN. Would you mind briefing me on it?

MAN. Not at all. *(Flips through pages.)* My target age is fifty, give or take a few years. I plan to start small, an expensive foreign sports car, some flashy clothes, a harmless infatuation with a much younger woman, not acted upon —

WOMAN. Such restraint. I'm impressed.

MAN. Well, you might want to withhold judgment, because then I thought I would move up to a serious affair of frightening intensity with an emotionally disturbed model or actress, leading to a temporary separation from my wife and family, several humiliating social episodes, some random drunkenness and maybe even a brief drug problem, all culminating in a life-or-death struggle for my very soul.

WOMAN. That's awfully dramatic.

MAN. I believe at that point, having worked as hard as I plan to, I will deserve it.

WOMAN. I could score some major sympathy points, as well as impressing others with my ability to hold up under such a scandal. My dignity index would soar.

MAN. Both men and women will look down upon me but secretly admire my impetuous and adventurous nature. Of course, if everything goes according to plan, I will realize the folly of my ways, and return to you with a new level of maturity, humility and respect for all that you offer me.

WOMAN. I, of course, will have suffered tremendously, and through your guilt will be able to get whatever I want from you until you die.

MAN. Naturally.

WOMAN. It's an attractive scenario ... but I'm worried about the effect it might have on the children.

MAN. Negligible. They should be hopelessly neurotic by that point, anyway.

WOMAN. You think?

MAN. Definitely. After years of private school, under constant pressure to succeed? They will be addicted to overachievement and equipped with completely unrealistic standards and unattainable goals.

WOMAN. Just like us!

MAN. Ulcers before they finish adolescence, you mark my words.

WOMAN. You're certainly optimistic.

MAN. You have to think big.

WOMAN. I must admit, I find your enthusiasm contagious.

MAN. Then shall I bring up the M word?

WOMAN. Before you do, may I be frank about something?

MAN. Please. *(Pause.)*

WOMAN. Sometimes you bore me so much I want to run screaming down a highway, naked, jabbing myself with hot needles, just to prove to myself that I am indeed alive, that I haven't drifted into some catatonic state resembling death but without its rewards.

MAN. Do you foresee this being a problem?

WOMAN. Oh, no. Quite the opposite. I can relax ... well, of course I can't really *relax*, I'm incapable of that, but — at least I know the day will never come when I suddenly discover that I have grown bored with you, and then descend into a melancholy period of, oh, two or three years, wondering where our lost love went. Such a scenario could be a severe setback. With you, I can avoid it altogether.

MAN. Very efficient.

WOMAN. And you know how I feel about efficiency.

MAN. Anything else?

WOMAN. No, I think you may proceed.

MAN. Well. I propose that you and I consider getting mar — *(He is unable to say it.)* Excuse me. I must have something in my throat. *(Indicating water.)* May I? *(He pours himself a glass of water and drinks.)* Let's try that again. I propose that you and I get mar — *(Again, he is unable to say it.)* Excuse me. *(He steps aside, and goes through some sort of athletic warmup ritual.)* I am stronger than I've ever been and getting stronger every day. I am stronger than I've ever been and getting stronger every day. I am stronger than I've ever been and getting stronger every day. *(Some intense breathing.)* I can do this. I am capable of this. I can argue persuasively, I can drive my point home, I can sell anything to anybody. *(He takes a deep breath and the faces the Woman, who has resumed working.)* I'm ready now.

WOMAN. Oh. *(She puts her work down and looks at him.)*

MAN. I propose that we get mar — *(Again, he is unable to say it.)* Damn. *(He pours another glass of water and douses his face with it. Blurting.)* Would you like to merge? *(Pause.)*

WOMAN. I would consider it.

MAN. Great. *(Handing her the document he entered with.)* I've taken the liberty of drawing up a preliminary proposal, outlining some of the things we've talked about. I'd like for you to read it, at your convenience, and then get back to me with your feedback.

WOMAN. May I make notes on this?

MAN. Of course, it's just a draft, and I have several copies.

WOMAN. Good. I'll get to it as soon as I can.

MAN. Great. *(Pause.)* I feel like we should do something to, you know, mark this occasion.

WOMAN. Like what?

MAN. Something celebratory.

WOMAN. Sex?

MAN. No, no, something faster. A toast, perhaps.

WOMAN. All right. *(She pours glasses of water. They toast.)*

MAN. To ... to the future.

WOMAN. To *our* future.

MAN. To *our* future. *(They drink. Checks his watch.)* Oh, my god. *(Grabs his notebook.)* Well, I hate to make a presentation and run, but I should have left thirty seconds ago. I'm really looking forward to hearing your comments on the proposal. May I call you on Monday?

WOMAN. Please do.

MAN. Okay! *(He leaves. The Woman waits until he's out of earshot. She then performs a brief, frantic, savage dance of joy before returning to her work.)*

BLACKOUT

PROPERTY LIST

Pitcher of water
Water glasses
Large document (MAN)
Personal notebook (MAN)

YOUR MOTHER'S BUTT

YOUR MOTHER'S BUTT was first produced by Alarm Dog Repertory at the West Bank Cafe Downstairs Theater Bar (Rand Foerster, Artistic Director), in New York City, on June 6, 1990. It was directed by Carol McCann. The cast was as follows:

CLIENT .... Barry Hamilton
PSYCHOLOGIST .... Terri O'Neil

CHARACTERS

PSYCHOLOGIST, woman, mid thirties
CLIENT, a young man

YOUR MOTHER'S BUTT

The Psychologist's office. The Psychologist, an intelligent, well-dressed woman in her mid-thirties, sits in a big comfortable chair, taking notes on a legal pad. Her Client lies on a couch, facing away from her. He is young, dressed artistically.

CLIENT. My life is like, so mundane. The days come, the days go. I keep waiting, waiting, waiting, but for what? I go to work, I eat, I work out. I watch television. I'm not really depressed. Well, yeah, I guess I am depressed. I'm lonely. I'm easily irritated. But it's not the kind of overwhelming depression that feels like it's ripping me apart. It's more of a ... blandness, an overall numbness ... like every fiber of my being has been sucked dry of any coherent reason to exist. *(Pause.)*
PSYCH. You're not enjoying your work?
CLIENT. Oh, God, no. Work is so weird. We're so busy right now, and there are so many things I'm responsible for, and all of them are meaningless. God. So much of my time is spent worrying about bullshit, manufacturing bullshit, packaging bullshit so it looks like it matters. Nothing matters.
PSYCH. Nothing?
CLIENT. *(Suddenly angry)* Nothing. And if it does, it just fucks you up. *(Pause.)*
PSYCH. So nothing in your life matters to you? *(Pause. The Client fights back tears.)*
CLIENT. No. *(Pause. The Client cries.)* I have — *(It is too painful for him to say; he takes a moment, then tries again.)* I have this sweater.
PSYCH. A sweater?
CLIENT. It's really nice. It's this old sweater, I think it be-

longed to my brother. It's just this black V-neck sweater, wool, but it's faded and soft and it fits me really well, it accentuates my shoulders, but like, in a subtle way, and when I wear it, I feel really sexy.

PSYCH. It sounds like a nice sweater.

CLIENT. It is. *(He breaks down)* I'm sorry, I just —

PSYCH. Take your time. *(Pause.)*

CLIENT. The reason I'm crying is that you ask me does anything really matter to me and my answer is a sweater? That's really sad.

PSYCH. You have every right to find joy in a sweater.

CLIENT. I do, that's the weird part, it's like the only thing in my life I get excited about. Sometimes I put it on just to walk around in it, and then sometimes I forget that I've done laundry and I go to pick out something to wear, and there it is, all clean and soft and faded just a little bit more, all folded up, and it's like, primal, like maybe even religious. *(Pause.)*

PSYCH. How are you feeling?

CLIENT. How do you think I'm feeling? The only significant relationship in my life is with a piece of clothing? At best, that's tremendously shallow and at worst, it's sociopathic. I mean, if I was somebody else and I knew me, I would say look, get a life.

PSYCH. I think perhaps you're being a bit hard on yourself.

CLIENT. You're right. God, I am so fucked up. I've got to do something about this, I can't be this fucked up any more. What can I do? Tell me what to do. You're the expert.

PSYCH. Well, first, I think we need to take a look at why you *are* so hard on yourself. *(Pause.)*

CLIENT. *(Sighs.)* Okay. *(Long pause.)*

PSYCH. How are you feeling?

CLIENT. Excited.

PSYCH. Excited?

CLIENT. Yeah. I'm thinking about this pair of shoes I saw yesterday.

PSYCH. Shoes?

CLIENT. Yeah. I've been looking for the perfect pair of black shoes for ... well, probably for my whole life. You know, a pair of oxfords, just plain, nice leather, not too clunky, but not too Wall Street, either. The kind of shoes you can wear with a suit and look really hip, but you can also wear with blue jeans and look really ... intelligent.

PSYCH. Intelligent.

CLIENT. But also approachable. And politically correct. With a sense of humor.

PSYCH. Shoes seem to communicate quite a lot for you.

CLIENT. Oh, yeah. Definitely. I think there's two ways to learn a lot about somebody in a short amount of time. One is their refrigerator — not only what they stick on the front of it, but what's in it, too — and the other is their shoes.

PSYCH. *(A hunch.)* What's in *your* refrigerator?

CLIENT. Well, nothing right now.

PSYCH. Ah.

CLIENT. These shoes are the greatest shoes — I *think.*

PSYCH. Let's stay with the image of the empty refrigerator for a moment.

CLIENT. Why?

PSYCH. I have an idea it might be significant.

CLIENT. Okay.

PSYCH. Just try to picture it. An empty box ... cold ... white ...

CLIENT. No, my refrigerator is avocado. *(Pause. The Psychologist seems disappointed.)*

PSYCH. Oh.

CLIENT. Which I really hate, because all the other appliances in my kitchen are harvest gold. Which I also hate, but I just haven't decided if I'm committed enough to this apartment to redecorate yet.

PSYCH. Let's just say, for argument's sake, that your refrigerator *was* white.

CLIENT. Okay.

PSYCH. *(Taking time, setting mood.)* A cold, white, empty box ... possibly a source of nourishment, but also a potential deathtrap. *(Pause.)*

CLIENT. Cool. *(Pause.)*

PSYCH. How are you feeling?

CLIENT. Weird. I think I just figured out what I really want.

PSYCH. What?

CLIENT. What I really want is to do the entire kitchen over in all black, with all black appliances ... but that really scares me.

PSYCH. Why?

CLIENT. Because in a few years, having had everything in your apartment be all black is going to be like having worn a leisure suit is today. It's going to be one of those things you'll have to constantly deny. You know, like I never voted for Reagan, I was never a yuppie. *(A long pause.)*

PSYCH. Perhaps we should return to the shoes.

CLIENT. Okay. *(Pause.)* I don't know. They might be the right ones, they might not. They're really expensive. I don't want to spend that much money and have them not be the perfect shoes! *(Suddenly angry.)* God, why does everything always have to be so hard?

PSYCH. Go ahead. Try to get in touch with this anger.

CLIENT. Sometimes I wish somebody would just tell me what to do, you know? They would just say, look, this is what you need to do, so just shut up and do it, okay? Because I don't seem to be able to figure it out on my own. It's like every option makes sense to me. Every choice seems like the right choice. Now, granted, I think being open-minded is a good thing, but there's such a thing as being *too* open-minded. Like your mind is so open it just kind of ... leaves.

PSYCH. Well, first, I think we need to look at the ways in which your indecision keeps you *safe* —

CLIENT. Oh, shut up! Just shut up! God! Stop telling me what to do! *(Looks at her, horrified, then bursts into tears.)* Oh God, I'm sorry! *(A very long pause.)*

PSYCH. How are you feeling?

CLIENT. I feel ... well, I'm not sure what I feel. I need to ask you a question. *(Pause.)*

PSYCH. All right.

CLIENT. And this not real easy for me, okay? *(Pause.)* Do you know where I can get a braided leather belt, about half an inch thick, black leather, not shiny, for under thirty dollars?

PSYCH. A belt?

CLIENT. Yeah. I have such bad luck with belts.

PSYCH. A belt?

CLIENT. Yes. *(Pause.)*

PSYCH. Were you ever ... what association does the word belt carry for you?

CLIENT. Ostrich.

PSYCH. Ostrich. A flightless bird, known primarily for sticking it's head in the ground in response to perceived danger —

CLIENT. No, I used to have these Eurotrash slip-on shoes, made out of ostrich skin? They were queer, but they were so incredibly soft. I just wanted to touch them all the time, even though I hardly ever wanted to wear them. So can you imagine a belt made out of ostrich skin, the softest stuff in the entire world? It would be like, intense.

PSYCH. Let me put it another way. When you were a child, and your parents felt they needed to punish you, for a perceived transgression ...

CLIENT. Oh, did they like, beat me?

PSYCH. Did they?

CLIENT. Well, sure, but not with a belt. With a switch.

PSYCH. Who?

CLIENT. A switch. From a tree.

PSYCH. Who used the switch?

CLIENT. Well, my mother. Of course.

PSYCH. Ah. *(Pause.)* How are you feeling?

CLIENT. Weird. I just remembered ... oh, I had this weird dream.

PSYCH. Tell me about it.

CLIENT. I dreamed ... I dreamed I was in this ... house, it wasn't my house, but I lived there. And I was in this big room, and I was in this bathtub. This old-fashioned bathtub on pedestals. And I'm wearing clothes. This olive drab cardigan, just over a T-shirt, and these flax-colored, I guess, linen shorts. No pleats. Really nice. Well, they would be, wouldn't they? Dream clothes. And then I hear these voices in the hall and in comes my mother. Only she's a younger version of herself, and she's wearing these 1960's hip-huggers, and she has Mary Tyler Moore hair that she's tied a bandana around, and I think oh, she's trying to be hip, and it's really sort of *sad* for a moment ... then she gets in the bathtub with me, only she won't look at me, and then she bends over and ... she just sticks her butt in my face.

PSYCH. *(Scribbling furiously.)* This is really good.

CLIENT. And I'm thinking ... okay. This is kind of weird. This is some weird kind of fuck-you gesture, and I'm thinking ... this is really ... it's really not quite right ... it's really ...

PSYCH. Inappropriate?

CLIENT. It's more than that.... Oh, God, what is it?

PSYCH. Visualize the dream.

CLIENT. Right.

PSYCH. You're in the water ... is the water warm or cold?

CLIENT. Warm. But not hot.

PSYCH. And she comes in.

CLIENT. Yeah, and she's walking this swingy, hippy kind of walk, and I think oh, God, my mother. I'm so embarrassed.

PSYCH. And she gets in the tub ...

CLIENT. You can tell she think's she's really groovy.

PSYCH. Now she's in the water with you ...

CLIENT. Yeah. And she is wearing the most hideous, Barbie, like flower power outfit.

PSYCH. She's turning around.

CLIENT. She looks like Samantha Stevens on acid.

PSYCH. She's bending over.

CLIENT. With this macrame belt. I am not kidding you.

PSYCH. She's bending —

CLIENT. Oh, wait a minute! I just realized something. Oh, wow. *(Pause.)*

PSYCH. Yes?

CLIENT. It makes such perfect sense, doesn't it.

PSYCH. What does?

CLIENT. I get my bad belt luck from her. It's heredity. *(Long pause.)*

PSYCH. *(Just the slightest bit of tightness.)* How are you feeling?

CLIENT. I feel great! If it's hereditary, then I don't have to feel guilty for it. I have no control over it, so it's not my fault. Right?

PSYCH. Well, not exactly, no. One of the underlying assumptions that the therapeutic process is based upon is that you *do* have control over your life.

CLIENT. No thanks. I don't want that kind of responsibility. *(Pause.)*

PSYCH. I'd like to get back to your mother's butt.

CLIENT. Please. Be my guest.

PSYCH. It's such a strong image, with so many potential implications. It could open many doors. So I'd like to try something a little ... unorthodox.

CLIENT. Oh, no. You're not going to stick *your* butt in my face, are you?

PSYCH. No, no. I just want you to close your eyes, and relax. Feel the warm water in the tub. Now try to picture your mother's butt.

CLIENT. Okay.

PSYCH. Do you see it?

CLIENT. Plain as day.

PSYCH. Now speak to it.

CLIENT. I'm sorry?

PSYCH. Speak to your mother's butt.

CLIENT. Oh, right.

PSYCH. Think of it as separate from your mother. As an entity of its own. If you could communicate with it, what would you say?

CLIENT. Get out of my face.

PSYCH. Perhaps it would be helpful if you gave it a name.

CLIENT. What do you mean?

PSYCH. If it had a name, what would it be?

CLIENT. You mean like a person's name?

PSYCH. Possibly.

CLIENT. Like ... Debbie?
PSYCH. Perhaps.
CLIENT. This is really weird.
PSYCH. Just try speaking to it by name.
CLIENT. Get out of my face, Debbie. Excuse me, Debbie, can you get out of my face? Thank you. Yo, Debbie. Get the fuck out of my face.
PSYCH. Maybe you'd like to yell at it.
CLIENT. Sure, why not. *(Yells.)* Debbie! Get the fuck out of my face, you bitch! And take that hideous macrame belt with you!
PSYCH. Now become the butt.
CLIENT. What?
PSYCH. If you were the butt, what would you say in response?
CLIENT. Uhm, I'm Debbie the butt, and you better shut up. Stop telling me what to do. This is a free country and I can be wherever I want. If you don't like me being in your face, then *you* leave.
PSYCH. Now respond as yourself.
CLIENT. Fuck you, you stupid butt. I was here first.
PSYCH. Keep going.
CLIENT. Oh yeah, well ... fuck you back.
PSYCH. Keep going.
CLIENT. I'm confused. Am I me or am I the butt?
PSYCH. Keep going!
CLIENT. But —
PSYCH. Don't turn away from this! We're right on the verge of something!
CLIENT. Uhm —
PSYCH. Don't hold back! Tell that butt *how you are feeling*!
CLIENT. *(Loses it.)* God! Shut up! Get out of my fucking face, get out of my fucking bathtub, get of my fucking life, you fucking butt! I hate you, I hate you, I hate your fucking guts! *(He sobs uncontrollably. Long pause.)*
PSYCH. How are you feeling now?
CLIENT. I feel like the biggest asshole in the universe. I'm

never telling you another dream again. But ... oh, wow. Wow. This is intense.

PSYCH. What?

CLIENT. Have you ever been hit with like, this realization, it's like something you always knew, but it's the first time you've ever really seen it so clearly? Oh this is so weird, it's like déjà vu.

PSYCH. What? *(The Client sits up and looks at her.)*

CLIENT. *(With great resolve.)* I don't care how expensive they are, I'm buying those shoes!

BLACKOUT

PROPERTY LIST

Note pad (PSYCHOLOGIST)
Pen or pencil (PSYCHOLOGIST)

NEW PLAYS

★ **BE AGGRESSIVE by Annie Weisman.** Vista Del Sol is paradise, sandy beaches, avocado-lined streets. But for seventeen-year-old cheerleader Laura, everything changes when her mother is killed in a car crash, and she embarks on a journey to the Spirit Institute of the South where she can learn "cheer" with Bible belt intensity. "…filled with lingual gymnastics…stylized rapid-fire dialogue…" –*Variety*. "…a new, exciting, and unique voice in the American theatre…" –*BackStage West*. [1M, 4W, extras] ISBN: 0-8222-1894-1

★ **FOUR by Christopher Shinn.** Four people struggle desperately to connect in this quiet, sophisticated, moving drama. "…smart, broken-hearted…Mr. Shinn has a precocious and forgiving sense of how power shifts in the game of sexual pursuit…He promises to be a playwright to reckon with…" –*NY Times*. "A voice emerges from an American place. It's got humor, sadness and a fresh and touching rhythm that tell of the loneliness and secrets of life…[a] poetic, haunting play." –*NY Post*. [3M, 1W] ISBN: 0-8222-1850-X

★ **WONDER OF THE WORLD by David Lindsay-Abaire.** A madcap picaresque involving Niagara Falls, a lonely tour-boat captain, a pair of bickering private detectives and a husband's dirty little secret. "Exceedingly whimsical and playfully wicked. Winning and genial. A top-drawer production." –*NY Times*. "Full frontal lunacy is on display. A most assuredly fresh and hilarious tragicomedy of marital discord run amok…absolutely hysterical…" –*Variety*. [3M, 4W (doubling)] ISBN: 0-8222-1863-1

★ **QED by Peter Parnell.** Nobel Prize-winning physicist and all-around genius Richard Feynman holds forth with captivating wit and wisdom in this fascinating biographical play that originally starred Alan Alda. "QED is a seductive mix of science, human affections, moral courage, and comic eccentricity. It reflects on, among other things, death, the absence of God, travel to an unexplored country, the pleasures of drumming, and the need to know and understand." –*NY Magazine*. "Its rhythms correspond to the way that people—even geniuses—approach and avoid highly emotional issues, and it portrays Feynman with affection and awe." –*The New Yorker*. [1M, 1W] ISBN: 0-8222-1924-7

★ **UNWRAP YOUR CANDY by Doug Wright.** Alternately chilling and hilarious, this deliciously macabre collection of four bedtime tales for adults is guaranteed to keep you awake for nights on end. "Engaging and intellectually satisfying…a treat to watch." –*NY Times*. "Fiendishly clever. Mordantly funny and chilling. Doug Wright teases, freezes and zaps us." –*Village Voice*. "Four bite-size plays that bite back." –*Variety*. [flexible casting] ISBN: 0-8222-1871-2

★ **FURTHER THAN THE FURTHEST THING by Zinnie Harris.** On a remote island in the middle of the Atlantic secrets are buried. When the outside world comes calling, the islanders find their world blown apart from the inside as well as beyond. "Harris winningly produces an intimate and poetic, as well as political, family saga." –*Independent (London)*. "Harris' enthralling adventure of a play marks a departure from stale, well-furrowed theatrical terrain." –*Evening Standard (London)*. [3M, 2W] ISBN: 0-8222-1874-7

★ **THE DESIGNATED MOURNER by Wallace Shawn.** The story of three people living in a country where what sort of books people like to read and how they choose to amuse themselves becomes both firmly personal and unexpectedly entangled with questions of survival. "This is a playwright who does not just tell you what it is like to be arrested at night by goons or to fall morally apart and become an aimless yet weirdly contented ghost yourself. He has the originality to make you feel it." –*Times (London)*. "A fascinating play with beautiful passages of writing…" –*Variety*. [2M, 1W] ISBN: 0-8222-1848-8

NEW PLAYS

★ **SHEL'S SHORTS by Shel Silverstein.** Lauded poet, songwriter and author of children's books, the incomparable Shel Silverstein's short plays are deeply infused with the same wicked sense of humor that made him famous. "...[a] childlike honesty and twisted sense of humor." –*Boston Herald.* "...terse dialogue and an absurdity laced with a tang of dread give [*Shel's Shorts*] more than a trace of Samuel Beckett's comic existentialism." –*Boston Phoenix.* [flexible casting] ISBN: 0-8222-1897-6

★ **AN ADULT EVENING OF SHEL SILVERSTEIN by Shel Silverstein.** Welcome to the darkly comic world of Shel Silverstein, a world where nothing is as it seems and where the most innocent conversation can turn menacing in an instant. These ten imaginative plays vary widely in content, but the style is unmistakable. "...[*An Adult Evening*] shows off Silverstein's virtuosic gift for wordplay...[and] sends the audience out...with a clear appreciation of human nature as perverse and laughable." –*NY Times.* [flexible casting] ISBN: 0-8222-1873-9

★ **WHERE'S MY MONEY? by John Patrick Shanley.** A caustic and sardonic vivisection of the institution of marriage, laced with the author's inimitable razor-sharp wit. "...Shanley's gift for acid-laced one-liners and emotionally tumescent exchanges is certainly potent..." –*Variety.* "...lively, smart, occasionally scary and rich in reverse wisdom." –*NY Times.* [3M, 3W] ISBN: 0-8222-1865-8

★ **A FEW STOUT INDIVIDUALS by John Guare.** A wonderfully screwy comedy-drama that figures Ulysses S. Grant in the throes of writing his memoirs, surrounded by a cast of fantastical characters, including the Emperor and Empress of Japan, the opera star Adelina Patti and Mark Twain. "Guare's smarts, passion and creativity skyrocket to awesome heights..." –*Star Ledger.* "...precisely the kind of good new play that you might call an everyday miracle...every minute of it is fresh and newly alive..." –*Village Voice.* [10M, 3W] ISBN: 0-8222-1907-7

★ **BREATH, BOOM by Kia Corthron.** A look at fourteen years in the life of Prix, a Bronx native, from her ruthless girl-gang leadership at sixteen through her coming to maturity at thirty. "...vivid world, believable and eye-opening, a place worthy of a dramatic visit, where no one would want to live but many have to." –*NY Times.* "...rich with humor, terse vernacular strength and gritty detail..." –*Variety.* [1M, 9W] ISBN: 0-8222-1849-6

★ **THE LATE HENRY MOSS by Sam Shepard.** Two antagonistic brothers, Ray and Earl, are brought together after their father, Henry Moss, is found dead in his seedy New Mexico home in this classic Shepard tale. "...His singular gift has been for building mysteries out of the ordinary ingredients of American family life..." –*NY Times.* "...rich moments ...Shepard finds gold." –*LA Times.* [7M, 1W] ISBN: 0-8222-1858-5

★ **THE CARPETBAGGER'S CHILDREN by Horton Foote.** One family's history spanning from the Civil War to WWII is recounted by three sisters in evocative, intertwining monologues. "...bittersweet music—[a] rhapsody of ambivalence...in its modest, garrulous way...theatrically daring." –*The New Yorker.* [3W] ISBN: 0-8222-1843-7

★ **THE NINA VARIATIONS by Steven Dietz.** In this funny, fierce and heartbreaking homage to *The Seagull*, Dietz puts Chekhov's star-crossed lovers in a room and doesn't let them out. "A perfect little jewel of a play..." –*Shepherdstown Chronicle.* "...a delightful revelation of a writer at play; and also an odd, haunting, moving theater piece of lingering beauty." –*Eastside Journal (Seattle).* [1M, 1W (flexible casting)] ISBN: 0-8222-1891-7